Then They Shall Know That I Am The Lord

The Unveiling of Our Lord Jesus Christ

By Stephen Temple

It is hoped that the words that immediately jump from the cover to the eye will bring to the reader's mind the central message of this book – "Know I Am Lord."   The subtitle is more subdued and is being "revealed" almost as if from within the clouds upon which the Son of Man said that He would come - a coming that would prove beyond doubt "That Jesus Christ is Lord, to the glory of the Father."

ISBN: 978-1535536257

Cover Design by:
Jeffrey T. McCormack
Apologia Book Shoppe
www.apologiabooks.com

Published by JaDon Management Inc.
1405 4th Ave. N. W.
#109
Ardmore, Ok., 73401

Table of Contents

Foreword

"What think ye of Christ? Whose Son is he?" (Matthew 22:42). Jesus' question to the Jews is one of the critical questions of not only theology, but indeed, of history itself! Controversy about the answer to that question has swirled since the birth of Christianity, and shows no signs of abating, as men and women reflect on this man, his birth, his life, his works, his ministry, his death and resurrection.

Jesus' contemporaries were puzzled and challenged by Jesus. They asked if Messiah would work more miracles, or greater miracles, than did Jesus. But, Jesus' miracles did not settle the question of who Jesus is, except to demonstrate that he was a prophet like other prophets who had performed miracles. His miracles alone did not, therefore, settle the question of who Jesus is. Even though John the Baptizer proclaimed, "I have seen and testified that this is the Son of God" (John 1:34), yet, the people were often perplexed as the Gospel of John testifies.

In stark contrast to other historical religious figures who resisted investigation of their claims, Jesus openly challenged his contemporaries to examine his life, his words, and most of all, his works: "If I do not do the works of My Father, do not believe Me; but if I do, though you do not believe Me, believe the works, that you may know and believe that the Father is in

Me, and I in Him" (John 10:37-38).

The resurrection of Jesus was one of those "works" that the Father gave him, and thus, he was, "declared to be the Son of God with power according to the Spirit of holiness, by the resurrection from the dead" (Romans 1:4). As Paul declared, if Christ was not raised from the dead, "our faith is vain, we are of all men most miserable." Indisputably, then, the fulfillment of Jesus' resurrection predictions is fundamental for our belief in Jesus as the Son of God. His resurrection stands unique among all other resurrections in scripture. Paul said Jesus was "the first to be raised from the dead." This stunning statement - when properly considered - challenges all views of the eschatological resurrection. John said that Jesus' physical resurrection was a sign, a *sign*, not of similar resurrections, *but of something else beyond and greater than the physical reality* (John 20:30-31)! The significance of this can hardly be over-emphasized, yet, it is mostly ignored.

The same is true of the parousia, what is commonly called the Second Coming, of Christ. The vast majority of Evangelical Christians, and historical Christianity, insist that one day Jesus will come out of the sky, riding on a cumulus cloud, as a 5'5" Jewish man, in a body of flesh and blood. But, that is not the Biblical view of the coming of Christ in spite of the popularity of that concept and in spite of how long that view has been preached. Far from it!

In this wonderful book, Stephen Temple sets before the reader some remarkable and irrefutable facts concerning Jesus' coming. Jesus said that his coming in judgment of all men would be "in the glory of the Father" (Matthew 16:27-28) and, he said that in his judgment / resurrection coming, he would act in the same way that he had seen the Father act!

Temple shares with us the indisputable fact that Jesus' promise to come in judgment "in the glory of the Father" meant that he was to come in judgment as the Father had come before. What many Bible students will find challenging is that the Father had come many times in the Old Testament Scriptures! Yet, He had never come in judgment in a literal descent out of heaven in a human form. He had, in exercise of His Divine Sovereignty, used one nation to judge another nation, such as when He used the Assyrians to judge Egypt (Isaiah 19-20). Like when He used the Assyrians to judge Israel (Isaiah 10). It was like when He used Nebuchadnezzar, the Babylonian king that He called "the sword in My hand' to judge Judah, Egypt, Tyre and Sidon (Ezekiel 29-32).

When YHVH sovereignly acted in history in this manner, it was called "the Day of the Lord." It was called the "coming of the Lord." He was said to come on the clouds, with flaming fire! In passage after passage, YHVH was said to, "come out of His place" to tread on the tops of the mountains, and destroy "heaven and earth." Lamentably, many Bible students are almost totally ignorant of this and see no connection with Jesus' predictions of his parousia / coming. Yet, that is *precisely* what Jesus said about his "Second Coming"! He was coming like the

Father had come! He would judge in the same manner that the Father had judged! And, there is something else here that Temple develops well.

In the Tanakh (the Old Testament) when God acted in history, He sent His prophets to the nation or people that He was about to judge. He sent those prophets to say that judgment was coming if they did not repent (See Jonah). Furthermore, in passage after passage, the prophet proclaiming that imminent judgment said that the Lord was going to act in judgment: "That they may know that I am God." This is a fundamentally important concept to grasp in order to understand the "Second Coming of Jesus."

As just noted, it is widely maintained in the futurist views of eschatology that Jesus will come again, in a human body of flesh. He will be revealed as a man once again. But, as Temple illustrates with excellent exegetical skill, that completely misses the point of the purpose of Jesus' coming! Jesus was not – is not - coming to be manifested once again "in the likeness of sinful flesh" or in his "body of humiliation."

Jesus was openly called the "son of God" by John the Baptizer, and this was more of an acclimation that he was a great man. Throughout his ministry Jesus taught his disciples and the Jews that he is "one greater than the Temple" (Matthew 12). As will be developed below, this, and many other statements that Jesus made were stunning, revolutionary! The Gospel of John tells us that Jesus' resurrection bears witness to the fact that he is the

Son of God, and Paul adds his voice to that in Romans. Indeed, the Jews understood well enough that Jesus made himself "equal with God" - and wanted to kill him for his claims. When Caiaphas asked Jesus if he is the Christ, the Son of the Living God, Jesus' (positive) response - with the attendant prediction of his coming on the clouds in judgment - elicited the immediate call for his death on the charge of blasphemy! The Sanhedrin knew full well what Jesus was claiming. He was claiming to be, "the King of kings and Lord of lords!"

What Temple does in this book is to set before the reader the indisputable and wide ranging evidence that Jesus' "second coming" was the final, consummative declaration, sign and proof that he truly is "the King of kings." Just as the Father's sovereign acts of judgment in the Tanakh was to show who He is: "That they may know that I am God", Temple shares with the readers that this is the same identical purpose for Jesus' coming. He would act in judgment in the same way the Father had acted, so that men might know who He is. Acting as the Father had acted, Jesus was not coming – at the risk of being redundant - as a man. He would use the judgment prerogative given to him by the Father. He would - and did - use that authority to judge the Old Covenant nation of Israel that had rejected him and put him to death. By using his divine sovereignty to bring the Romans against Old Covenant Jerusalem in AD 70, Jesus was indeed manifested as "King of kings and Lord of lords."

It is high time that the modern church put aside the materialistic concepts of the Day of the Lord, the very concepts that led to the rejection and death of Jesus at the hands of the Jews. They had a false concept of the nature of the kingdom and Messiah. Thus, when Jesus did not meet those expectations, they rejected him. Likewise, the modern church has imposed a physical, material concept of the nature of the "Second Coming" onto the text, and as a result has failed– sometimes refused - to see that, just as the disciples understood in Matthew 24 - the fall of Jerusalem was the sign of the parousia (presence) of Jesus in his role as "The Son of God" coming "in power and great glory." It is a miscarriage of exegesis to expect and anticipate the coming of Jesus on literal clouds, as a man in a body of flesh. It is time to see Him in his Divine judgment actions in AD 70, "in the glory of the Father," and thereby to, "know that I am God."

I urge a careful, thoughtful reading of this excellent book.

Don K. Preston
President, Preterist Research Institute
Ardmore, Ok. 73401
www.eschatology.org
www.bibleprophecy.com
www.donkpreston.com

Then They Shall Know That I Am The Lord

The Unveiling of Our Lord Jesus Christ

Introduction

Much has been written about various aspects of what is commonly called the Second Coming of Jesus Christ, and this event can be looked at from a number of different perspectives. While nowhere specifically or explicitly called "the Second Coming" (although Hebrews 9:28 says that, *"He will appear a second time"*), this "event" is described in numerous New Testament passages and is agreed to be the focal point of a multitude of Old and New Testament prophecies. It could and should be argued that Christ would accomplish and fulfill several different purposes with and through this second coming. He would pour out judgment against His enemies, He would bring about deliverance for His elect, He would consummate the New Covenant through the final fulfillment of all God's promises to Israel of old, and He would manifest Himself in a way that would fully demonstrate that He was the Son of God and that He was Lord, to the glory of God the Father. This final aspect will be the primary focus of this work.

Some readers may wonder where this last stated purpose above is actually spelled out in the scriptures. Many passages will be discussed in this work, but one significant New Testament book has it as its primary focus. The book of Revelation deals with the unveiling of Jesus. Although at times difficult for many (including the likes of Martin Luther) to fully comprehend, when properly understood this

1

text reveals an understanding of Jesus' full identify in a way that was not as completely developed by any of the other New Testament documents. There are however, certainly many Old and New Testament passages that will also be critical to this overall investigation. In fact we can emphatically state that the book of Revelation does not stand by itself, and that it is indeed as much, if not more dependent upon the Old Testament scriptures as any other of the New Testament documents.

Obviously there is much disagreement throughout the many different religions of the world, and even among the "non-religious", regarding the identity of Jesus of Nazareth. Most would agree that Jesus was a historical figure, and even Islam's sacred book the Koran speaks of Him as one sent from God as one of the great prophets. In his book *Reading Backwards*, New Testament scholar Richard B. Hays works to demonstrate that the canonical Gospels portray Jesus as much more than just a great man. On page 19, he states the following: "We can understand why it is not sufficient to interpret Jesus as a great prophet or even as the expected Davidic king, for he is one who is still greater. The categories of prophet and messiah are not wrong, but they fail to do full justice to his identity." It is the purpose of the following discussion to demonstrate that Jesus made claims to be one with God and how it was that He ultimately demonstrated/manifested the truth of His full identity, showing that He was in fact equal with God.

There are many wonderful studies (one such study is noted at the very end of this book) available that thoroughly discuss the manifold evidence that the New Testament writers use language and images in speaking of Jesus, that clearly point back to Old Testament descriptions and images of Israel's God. These studies are very important and help establish that Jesus and the New Testament

2

writers were firmly convinced of Jesus' status as Son of God, but this does not in itself provide proof positive of the truthfulness of their convictions.

To make a claim is one thing, but to conclusively demonstrate it to be true is quite another. I would use the word vindicate to describe the process which Jesus would follow to accomplish this goal. In our world today, a primary meaning of this word is "to show that someone or something that has been criticized or doubted is correct, true, or reasonable." This matter is of greatest importance not just to Christians, but to all the family of man.

Before moving forward with this study and in order to ensure that readers of this material are clear on the issues being discussed, let me provide the definition of several important terms before getting into the meat of our topic. These definitions along with that of other related terms are provided on Don K. Preston's website at: http://www.eschatology.org/index.php?option=com_content&v iew=article&id=235:glossary-of-terms&amp&Itemid=61

No doubt there are those who may find that they disagree with certain aspects or points contained in these definitions, but what is presented below provides a reference and a context for what is considered in much of the following study.

Eschatology: This is a compound Greek word formed from *eschatos*, meaning last, and the suffix (ending), meaning the study of. Thus, eschatology is the study of the last things which normally includes the Second Coming of Christ, the Judgment and Resurrection. Many people think of the end of time or the end of human history as we know it when they think of the term the last days, or the time of the end. However, the Bible defines the last days and eschatology as a reference to the last days of Old Covenant Israel, and eschatology as being a reference to the end of Israel's Old Covenant Age. The time of the end was the first century generation, which was the end of Israel's Covenant Age.

Preterist/ Preterism: This word is actually from the Latin word meaning past. The idea, when applied to eschatology, is that all prophecy has been fulfilled in the past. Thus, in opposition to the other views of eschatology that place the parousia (second coming of Christ) and judgment in the future, preterism places it in the past, in the lifetime of Jesus' first century generation (Matthew 16:27-28).

Covenant Eschatology: This term refers to the idea that the Biblical story of eschatology has to do with the last days of the Old Covenant World of Israel that came to an end in A.D. 70, with the fall of Jerusalem. Most views of eschatology believe that Biblical eschatology deals with the end of human history as we know it. In other words, Historical Eschatology, the end of history. Covenant Eschatology on the other hand, believes that Biblical eschatology deals with the end of the Covenant History of Israel, i.e. Covenant Eschatology.

Let me emphasize here that in this view, the end of Israel's Old Covenant age coincided with the consummation of the promised New Covenant age.

From my perspective, one additional comment is appropriate as this study begins. I came across a comment made by a Christian brother named John Shakespeare who lives in Walsall, England. At the beginning of a study on a different topic, he made the following comments that well express my own personal feelings: "Before I start this, I just want to say that I am very concerned about it. I am

4

desperately anxious not to mislead you, or to be a false teacher. So I ask you to think carefully about our role together as the pillar and ground of truth. Don't let me get away with anything. Search the Scriptures with extreme care to check what I say." I believe that the biblical texts drawn upon in the subsequent study will fully support the assertions, interpretations and conclusions put forth here, but if you feel convinced that there is error present, please provide a scripturally based response explaining what you perceive to be in error. Please do so in a loving and respectful manner. Feel free to disagree, but let us always treat one another as fellow members of Christ's body.

Timing: When Did Jesus Say He Would Come?

The tenets of Covenant Eschatology (otherwise known as preterism) must certainly seem incredible and bizarre to those who hold to any futurist eschatology and who have no previous exposure to them. When a person has heard for much of their life that we are now in the last days and that Jesus is coming soon, it is perplexing to say the least when exposed to the proposition that these things actually happened in the 1st century.

Having read through the Bible multiple times in years past, I personally was taken aback when first hearing a presentation that focused on some of the many statements pointing to a 1st century fulfillment of events I had always understood as still future. As I began to read more carefully (at least with regard to awareness of these statements), it soon became obvious that the statements of imminence (temporal nearness) were not just found in a few isolated and sparsely dispersed passages, but were pervasive throughout the New Testament. As hard as it was to accept a teaching so profoundly different from what I had previously believed, it was ultimately even harder to reject the many explicit scriptural statements of imminent fulfillment, and numerous others that are perhaps somewhat less direct or explicit, but which were still quite clear.

There are certainly Christians who have had some exposure to preterist teachings and who, while acknowledging that there are passages with an apparent sense of imminence, remain personally convinced that the fulfilled paradigm is false. More and more however, others are coming to see a pattern that they cannot ignore or reject, and although in many ways struggling with the traditions of the historic church or the teachings of their own particular

6

denominations, have reached a point of conviction that these many time statements must be taken seriously.

There are still others, classified as partial preterists, who acknowledge and strongly profess that many New Testament eschatological passages did indeed find fulfillment in what took place in and around Jerusalem circa AD70. But they also believe that there are other prophetic passages which will be fulfilled sometime in our future. Historically, many who hold to this position have chosen to call themselves preterists. Indeed before those who were more *consistently* preterist in their views began to become more visible, those generally called preterists were in fact ones who are today frequently called partial preterists.

In many ways a very positive thing, there seems to be a growing emphasis in many churches on individual Bible reading with plans abounding to guide believers as they seek to read through the Bible over the course of a year. Some of these formalized plans however, have readers jumping about, following patterns that give no apparent acknowledgment to the covenantal historical flow found within the Old and New Testaments. In many instances, little emphasis is placed on trying to understand what these texts actually meant to those who originally received them. When statements are read in the New Testament that refer to something that is to happen soon, it is common to see them as referring to our day instead of recognizing that the message was specifically addressed to people alive almost two thousand years ago. This not only occurs with individual personal Bible reading, but it is often reinforced by teachers and preachers whose influence bears considerable weight in the minds of many who hear their words.

Bible commentator Tony Denton had this to say regarding the importance of covenant in the overall biblical scheme: "Scripture came into being as an expression of the relationship between God and His people, a relationship that the Bible typically portrays in terms of a covenant. Every issue in the Bible ends up somehow finding its meaning within the ebb and flow of the covenant relationship between the Lord and His people; in this sense, covenant is the air that Scripture breathes, supplying the framework for understanding all parts of the Old and New Testaments." [1] Please keep these thoughts in mind as you read through what follows.

Probably the main reason for this is that audience relevance as a concept is seldom mentioned or discussed. It is common to hear people claim that the Bible was written to those of us living in the 21st century. While I would not deny at all that the New Testament scriptures have great relevance to our lives, I would most certainly reject the idea that they were written to anyone other than those in Jesus' 1st century generation. Take for instance the opening words of Luke's gospel.

"Inasmuch as many have taken in hand to set in order a narrative of those things which have been fulfilled among us, just as those who from the beginning were eyewitnesses and ministers of the word delivered them to us, it seemed good to me also, having had perfect understanding of all things from the very first, to write to you an orderly account, most

---

[1]

http://tfcmag.com/preview1.php?id=125&p=3&search=Tony+Denton

excellent Theophilus, that you may know the certainty of those things in which you were instructed" (Luke 1:1-4).

Luke stated specifically that he was writing to Theophilus who as far as we know, lived in the 1st century. The same applies to the book of Acts. Without exception the New Testament epistles (including Revelation) were addressed to specific contemporary people or groups of people. All these writers had a message of vital importance for those in their own generation. Certainly they are important to us as well, but the sense of urgency and imminence that permeates these documents cannot rightfully be transferred 2000 years into the future. When James wrote to a specific people and said to them that "the Lord's coming is near," and that "the Judge is standing at the door," he was not talking to 21st century America or anyone else in the 21st century world. We need always to understand as best we can what the words of the Bible writers meant to their 1st century readers.

A speaker at a conference I attended several years ago spoke on the resurrection of the dead from the perspective of premillennial eschatology. Throughout his presentation he emphasized the fact that many of the New Testament passages referring to resurrection refer to it as a future event. He reasoned from this that as we in the 21st century read the New Testament scriptures, this future tense must still apply to us. Few if any would deny that the resurrection is addressed as a future event in much of the New Testament literature. We must ask ourselves, however, whether the fact that the resurrection was seen as a future event within the 1st century epistles necessarily calls for it to be a future to us occurrence. Simply because the 1st century writers used the future tense does not necessarily mean that the events that they wrote about must still be future to us, especially considering the overriding sense of imminent expectation pervading these texts.

Theoretically it is possible that they are, but it does not logically follow that as we read them today, they must be still future.

The question I am posing at this point is not whether the resurrection has actually occurred, but rather does the future tense used by 1st century writers require that the event they were writing about be a still future event almost 2000 years later? This would be somewhat analogous to reading a letter that George Washington had written to his wife in 1780 in which he talks about a battle that he anticipated taking place in his immediate future, and then asserting that as we read it today it is still future to us simply because he wrote about it using the future tense. Certainly all of us understand that if the battle happened as anticipated, then our reading and understanding of his letter in our day must be conditioned by that fact.

Likewise, despite the fact that most modern Christians would vehemently deny that the resurrection spoken of in the New Testament is past, can't we agree at least in principle that if it had already happened this would significantly impact our understanding of the future tense statements found in the New Testament? Simply put then, the grammar of the New Testament does not require that the future events it describes still be future to us today. They could indeed be, but this is not required to be simply because of the forward looking nature of the 1st century writings.

Without a doubt, the "church" has an inglorious history of failed predictions regarding Christ's second coming. Hundreds (perhaps thousands!) have been made, and these prognosticators have been condemned by others who say that the Bible says no one knows the day or hour when He shall come. History would seem to tell us that these predictions will continue to be made and I believe will continue

10

to fail, not because no one can know "when" Christ will come, but because they fail to take into account that Jesus and the other New Testament writers were speaking primarily and specifically to that 1st century generation.

There is in fact a great deal of information in the New Testament that would help the 1st century saints know when their Lord would come. Jesus went to great pains to give *them* signs to watch for that would signify that the time was near. *They* were to watch for these signs so that *they* would not be caught by surprise. Although He did not tell them the exact day and hour that He would come, Jesus did clearly delimit a general time frame in which this event would occur: "this generation."

To say that because Jesus said: "Of that day and hour no one knows, not even the angels of heaven, but My Father only," means that no one at that time can know, "when" He will come, is true in one sense. It is true that at the time He made the statement no one could know the specific time and date, but that is not the same thing as saying that no one could have any idea at all when He would come. This is especially true considering that He had just told His disciples that, "this generation will by no means pass away till all these things take place." "These things" included, "the Son of Man coming on the clouds of heaven with power and great glory."

The principle is the same as if I left in February on an extended business trip and told my wife that I did not know exactly when I would return, but that I was certain that it would be by the end of the year. Although my wife did not know the precise day and hour of my return, she knew that if I were faithful to my word I would be home at the latest by the end of December. If for some reason January 1st rolled around and I had not returned, then my wife would have good

11

reason to believe that I had lied to her. If Jesus did not return before that generation passed away, wouldn't it be correct to say that He had lied to His disciples? Most Christians would certainly be very reluctant to make such an accusation, but the strength and logic of this argument is hard to resist.

Now if I had called or written my wife in November and told her that my plans had changed and that my return was being delayed, at least I showed her some consideration by notifying her of the delay. This may not boost her confidence in the dependability of my words, but at least I showed some consideration for her feelings. We have no such statement from Christ saying that there would be a delay in His coming. If this delay continued to happen over and over, month by month, and year by year, her trust in my faithfulness would have vanished completely a long, long time ago.

Those who deny that Jesus returned in the 1st century do not even give Him credit for being considerate enough to let His people know that He was not coming as expected. The only way that those 1st century saints would have known that Jesus was not coming was because of the fact that He did not appear as promised. How disillusioned they must have been if in fact He did not return, and this has continued on through subsequent generations as he continues, according to the futurist perspective, to be a "no- show" without a word of explanation to those in each generation who anxiously await His "glorious appearing."

Understanding that one purpose of His coming was to be the judgment of those who did not love His appearing and the deliverance of those who did, we can find examples in the Old Testament where God stated His intention to judge a people but relented for various reasons. In these situations God made it plain that

12

He was not going to follow through with His original plan and stated the reason why he had relented. In all these cases He communicated His change in purpose. He was not just a no-show with no an explanation.

Perhaps the most prominent example that comes to my mind would be God's dealings with Nineveh as described in the book of Jonah. God's stated intention, as relayed through the prophet Jonah, was to come in judgment against the wicked people of Nineveh; however, because of their repentance in response to Jonah's preaching, God relented: "Then God saw their works, that they turned from their evil way; and God relented from the disaster that He had said He would bring upon them, and He did not do it" (Jonah 3:10).

God is merciful, gracious and extremely longsuffering. His grace was manifested repeatedly when He sent prophets to warn a people of His displeasure and called them to repentance. As stated by the prophet Amos: "The Lord God does nothing, unless He reveals His secret to His servants the prophets" (Amos 3:7). God made plain through Jeremiah that, "the instant I speak concerning a nation and concerning a kingdom, to pluck up, to pull down, and to destroy it, if that nation against whom I have spoken turns from its evil, I will relent of the disaster that I thought to bring upon it" (Jeremiah 18:7-8). Again, God is merciful and may relent from His originally stated purpose, but if He does so, we can be assured that it would be revealed through "His servants the prophets."

God's frustration with Israel was evident early on in the history of the nation, and in Exodus chapter 32 it appeared that God had reached the limit of His patience. He told Moses: "I have seen this people, and indeed it is a stiff-necked people! Now therefore, let Me alone, that My wrath may burn hot against them and I may consume them"

(Exodus 32:9-10). Moses then stood before the Lord and interceded for this "stiff-necked people." In verse 14, God responded to Moses' pleas. "So the LORD relented from the harm which He said He would do to His people." Here God diverged from His original intention to destroy these people. We know this because He clearly expressed His "change of heart" through Moses. He did not just change His mind and "walk" away without telling anyone.

This principle is also expressed in God's dealing with King Hezekiah. God sent the prophet Isaiah to Hezekiah with the following message: "Thus says the LORD: 'Set your house in order, for you shall die, and not live'" (2 Kings 20:1). Hezekiah's response was to humble himself and plead for God's mercy. God heard his prayer. He could have ignored his cries or He could have changed His mind and left Hezekiah on the tiptoe of expectation that He was about to die. Perhaps this would have motivated him to greater obedience and a heightened sense of duty to God. That, however, would have been out of character for God and that is not how He chose to respond to Hezekiah. Instead He sent Isaiah back to him with these words: "Thus says the LORD, the God of David your father: 'I have heard your prayer, I have seen your tears; surely I will heal you. On the third day you shall go up to the house of the LORD. And I will add to your days fifteen years. I will deliver you and this city from the hand of the king of Assyria; and I will defend this city for My own sake, and for the sake of My servant David'" (2 Kings 20:5-6). God could have kept Hezekiah in the dark; He could have kept him hanging, but according to all that the Bible teaches, that is not His way.

It is impossible to believe that Jesus would make so very plain His purpose to come in judgment within that first century time-frame (it was not simply a matter of time, but a specific group of people as well), and then not come without explaining the reason for His delay

14

or change in purpose. To me it is unconscionable to even infer that God would do such a thing, and this in essence is precisely what the futurist position does. Some deny that Jesus or the New Testament writers intended that their listeners believe that He was coming in their generation. Most however, recognize the language of imminence but try to explain why He did not come when He said He would.

In 1999 John MacArthur wrote a book titled *The Second Coming*. He wrote this book specifically to counter the increasing popularity of the Preterist or fulfilled eschatology position. He acknowledges that the New Testament is clear in teaching the imminence of Christ's return. His explanation for the prevalence of these time statements indicating imminence was that they were to keep Christians of all succeeding generations on the tiptoe of expectation ("He desired to keep His people on the tiptoe of expectation, continually looking for Him" (p.206)). This truly amounts to accusing God of intentional deception. We certainly find no example of God behaving in such a manner in the Old Testament historical accounts.

It can sometimes be dangerous and certainly irresponsible to take an isolated passage or verse of scripture and remove it from its context. There is a verse from Proverbs that may speak significantly to MacArthur's specific argument: "Hope deferred makes the heart sick, but when the desire comes, it is a tree of life" (Proverbs 13:12). By taking a look at a New Testament verse that most would agree refers to Jesus' second coming, we may see how this verse from Proverbs might speak to MacArthur's reasoning (understanding that MacArthur is not alone in teaching this perspective).

Paul wrote a letter to Titus that addressed contemporary conditions and expectations, and in a very familiar passage has this to say: "For the grace of God that brings salvation has appeared to all men, teaching us that, denying ungodliness and worldly lusts, we should live soberly, righteously, and godly in the present age, looking for the blessed hope and glorious appearing of our great God and Savior Jesus Christ, who gave Himself for us that He might redeem us from every lawless deed and purify for Himself His own special people, zealous for good works" (Titus 2:11-14). Some might take this passage as a perfect example of MacArthur's rationale that generation after generation would take it and others like it, as an exhortation to live godly in expectation of His glorious appearing. Were it not addressed specifically to 1st century saints, and had Paul perhaps made clear that it could be many generations into the future before the time of this glorious appearing, perhaps MacArthur's principle could be granted as valid. Paul however, made it clear that the blessed hope was specifically something that he and those to whom he wrote were to be looking for. It was their blessed hope, not ours nor any generation subsequent to theirs.

If Christ did not appear in that generation, then it is certain that many would have been sick of heart, and as this appearing was delayed generation after generation, this sickness of heart would have continued to grow through each succeeding generation. On the other hand, if Jesus (the desire of men's hearts) came as He said He would, then it would have been as a tree of life to them. It would have meant that He had redeemed them from every lawless deed and purified them as His own special people. The implication of Paul's words to Titus is that if Jesus' glorious appearing has not occurred, believers today have not been redeemed from every lawless deed and have not been purified as His own special people. The idea of hope is pervasive throughout the New Testament writings and therefore it

16

was pervasive in the minds of the 1st century believers as well. It is very difficult to believe that God has deferred this hope for almost 2000 years. What they hoped for in the 1st century, all subsequent generations of Christians, including our own, now possess.

To be fair to MacArthur, it should be noted that he does qualify the above statement by stating the following: "It is not that He desires each succeeding generation to believe that He will certainly return in their lifetime for He does not desire our faith and our practices to be founded on error, as in that case, the faith and practice of all generations except the last would be. But it is a necessary element of the doctrine concerning (the Second Coming of Christ) that it should be possible at any time, that no generation should consider it improbable as theirs (Archbishop Trench)" (p.207).

The problem with MacArthur's reasoning is that the words of Jesus and the New Testament writers are not open ended statements without definite time limitations. All the statements that deal with the timing of Jesus' coming refer to that present generation or specifically to those 1st century believers to whom the documents were written. There was no "maybe", but rather a definite expectation and a definite promise that the present (1st century) generation would not pass away until all, including the second coming, occurred.

This should indeed be a very important point of concern for the professing Christian who has placed his trust in the faithfulness of God. I think it may be helpful to look at an early example of God's way of fulfilling His promises.

In Genesis chapter 12, the familiar promise was made to Abram: "I will make you a great nation; I will bless you and make your name great; and you shall be a blessing" (Genesis 12:7). Here was a broad

17

general promise given with few if any specifics regarding exactly how and when this promise would be realized. One thing is certain however, the promise was made to Abram and he believed God and responded by departing from his home in Haran and going to Canaan. As time passed and Abram had no son, he began to wonder how God would accomplish His purpose to make him a great nation. The story continued in chapter 15, as God came to Abram.

> "After these things the word of the LORD came to Abram in a vision, saying, 'Do not be afraid, Abram. I am your shield, your exceedingly great reward.' But Abram said, 'Lord GOD, what will You give me, seeing I go childless, and the heir of my house is Eliezer of Damascus?' Then Abram said, 'Look, You have given me no offspring; indeed one born in my house is my heir!' And behold, the word of the LORD came to him, saying, 'This one shall not be your heir, but one who will come from your own body shall be your heir.' Then He brought him outside and said, 'Look now toward heaven, and count the stars if you are able to number them.' And He said to him, 'So shall your descendants be'" (Genesis 15:1-5).

Here again, God reaffirmed His promise, and yet there was still no specific timeframe given; only that his heir would come from his own body. Twenty-five years passed and Abraham still had no son. Once again God spoke to him:

> "'As for Sarai your wife, you shall not call her name Sarai, but Sarah shall be her name. And I will bless her and also give you a son by her; then I will bless her, and she shall be a mother of nations; kings of peoples shall be from her.' Then Abraham fell on his face and laughed, and said in his heart,

'Shall a child be born to a man who is one hundred years old? And shall Sarah, who is ninety years old, bear a child?' And Abraham said to God, 'Oh, that Ishmael might live before You!' Then God said: 'No, Sarah your wife shall bear you a son, and you shall call his name Isaac; I will establish My covenant with him for an everlasting covenant, and with his descendants after him. And as for Ishmael, I have heard you. Behold, I have blessed him, and will make him fruitful, and will multiply him exceedingly. He shall beget twelve princes, and I will make him a great nation. But My covenant I will establish with Isaac, whom Sarah shall bear to you at this set time next year'" (Genesis 17:15-21).

As God's designated time approached, He announced that Isaac would be born in a year. He had now given Abraham a specific timeframe. Chapter 21 presents the fact that Sarah bore Isaac at the "set time of which God had spoken to him." "And the LORD visited Sarah as He had said, and the LORD did for Sarah as He had spoken. For Sarah conceived and bore Abraham a son in his old age, at the set time of which God had spoken to him. And Abraham called the name of his son who was born to him-whom Sarah bore to him-Isaac" (Genesis 21:1-3). God's faithfulness is clearly presented in this passage. He made a promise to Abraham, but initially gave him no information as to when; the only thing that was certain was that the promise was to Abram. As the time grew near, God gave him more specific information which more closely pinpointed the fulfillment of God's promise.

In Deuteronomy 18:15-18, Moses pointed to the coming prophet who we now know to be Jesus. In the verses immediately following this prophecy we find these words from Yahweh:

19

"But the prophet who presumes to speak a word in My name, which I have not commanded him to speak, or who speaks in the name of other gods, that prophet shall die.' And if you say in your heart, "How shall we know the word which the LORD has not spoken?'-- when a prophet speaks in the name of the LORD, if the thing does not happen or come to pass, that is the thing which the LORD has not spoken; the prophet has spoken it presumptuously; you shall not be afraid of him" (Deuteronomy 18:20-22).

Skeptics point to the "failed" predictions of Jesus. Rachel Zurer, says "to spend almost two millennia trying to justify a pagan mythology, a mistaken messiah belief, and a mistaken eschatology stupefies the rational mind" (*A Jew Examines Christianity*. 1985, 162). Even those within Christianity, from the early centuries up until the present, have denied the truthfulness of the scriptures in large part because of the denial, even within the church. For example one of the more notable Christian scholars said: "Jesus' expectation of the near end of the world turned out to be an illusion."[2]

Far too often, even the words of Christians make Him out to be a false prophet, and the "world" stands by and watches as our attempts to explain away His words belittle and demean our precious Lord and Savior. Would that the church would stand up and proclaim the truth of God's words; proclaim that indeed Israel's Old Covenant house was left to them desolate; proclaim that not one stone was left upon another; proclaim that upon that "brood of vipers" came "all the

---

[2] Rudolph Bultman, *Theology in the New Testament*, (Vol. 1. 1961), 22.

righteous blood shed on the earth, from the blood of righteous Abel to the blood of Zechariah, son of Berechiah, whom you murdered between the temple and the altar" (Matthew 23:35).

These things were accomplished, and this was the very reason Jesus came in judgment of that "faithless and perverse generation." That generation had filled up the measure of their father's sin and God poured out the full measure of His cup of wrath upon them. Jesus came in His Father's glory. He came in judgment of those who Paul called the "enemies of the cross of Christ" (Philippians 3:18). God cannot lie and Jesus did not lie when He said that, "this generation will by no means pass away till all these things take place." Rather than being a cause for skepticism, the fulfillment of Jesus' prophetic promises should be a startling confirmation of the truth of Christianity. When one as a believer does come to see these things as true, it is quite riveting and exciting to finally understand that God in His Son Jesus Christ had faithfully fulfilled His promises within the generation that He said would receive them.

The supposed non-occurrence in the 1st century of the events prophesied by Jesus and the New Testament writers is a major source of ammunition for those who would attack the truth claims of Christianity. Whether atheist, Moslem or Jew, they recognize that Jesus plainly said He was coming in the 1st century. Interestingly they are in agreement with the majority of Christians today when they say that Jesus did not come in the 1st century, but in their minds, His non-appearance overwhelmingly condemns Jesus as a fraud - certainly He was not the Son of God, and therefore Christianity is proven false. The impact of the denial of His 1st century appearing does not stop with those who come against the church from the outside.

21

Many today rightly decry the low view of the Scriptures found in much of academia and even within many modern mainline protestant denominations. Some in these denominations no longer hold to the infallibility and inerrancy of the Bible. There is little doubt that underlying this, at least in part, is the belief that Jesus did not come in the 1st century as He said He would (see the quote from Bultman above). These have only taken this denial to its logical conclusion: the Bible is not the inspired word of God. Only the affirmations of fulfillment by those adhering to Covenant Eschatology can effectively counter those attacks against Jesus the Christ and His church. Many within the church have made valiant attempts to explain why the many seemingly obvious statements of our Lord did not really mean what they so clearly appear to say. The opponents and critics, both within and without the church, of the truthfulness of God's word see these efforts as futile and vain.

Many have taken Jesus' statement in Matthew 24:36 where He said, "But of that day and hour no one knows, not even the angels of heaven, but My Father only," as somehow countermanding or contradicting His earlier statement in v. 34. But all He was saying here is that at that time no one but the Father knew the precise time of His coming. He went on to compare the circumstances of His coming to those of the days of Noah. "But as the days of Noah were, so also will the coming of the Son of Man be. For as in the days before the flood, they were eating and drinking, marrying and giving in marriage, until the day that Noah entered the ark, and did not know until the flood came and took them all away, so also will the coming of the Son of Man be" (Matthew 24:37-39). What is the connection here? It is clear that God told Noah that He was going to do something, and that Noah was then to respond as directed by God. "And God said to Noah, 'The end of all flesh has come before Me, for the earth is filled with violence through them; and behold, I will

destroy them with the earth. Make yourself an ark of gopherwood'"
(Genesis 6:13-14).

God told Noah that He was going to destroy all flesh and that Noah
should therefore build an ark. He had told Noah earlier that he would
"not strive with man forever", and that "his days shall be one hundred
and twenty years" (verse 3). God gave Noah a general timeframe in
which this destruction would take place, just as Jesus did with His
disciples by telling them of things would happen within their
generation. He did not tell them precisely when He was coming, but
His statement made it plain that it would be confined to their
generation. Why else would He say to His disciples, "Watch
therefore, for you do not know what hour your Lord is coming"
(Matthew 24:42). Why would *they* need to watch if Jesus wasn't
coming in their lifetime? Likewise, why would God tell Noah to
build an ark if the all flesh destroying flood wasn't going to take place
in his lifetime? In Genesis 6:3, God spoke of the destruction of man.
He said that their days would be one hundred and twenty years, but he
did not tell him the hour or the day that it would take place.

Interestingly, God gave Noah more detailed information as the time
of the great cataclysm approached. In Genesis 7:4, God said: "For
after seven more days I will cause it to rain on the earth forty days and
forty nights, and I will destroy from the face of the earth all living
things that I have made." It can be seen therefore that God gave Noah
more precise information immediately prior to the coming of the
flood. So although Jesus did not give more specific information to
His disciples prior to His ascension, He did in fact give them
additional revelation at a later time. The book of Revelation is, in its
essence, Jesus making known that, "which God gave Him to show
His servants things which must shortly take place" (Revelation 1:1).

23

Many similarities are found between how God revealed His purposes to Noah and how Jesus revealed His to the disciples. Even in Noah's day when God had "condemned the world" (Hebrews 11:7), He was longsuffering with that generation (1 Peter 3:20). When Peter addressed those scoffers who asked, "Where is the promise of His coming?" (2 Peter 3:4), his response was almost identical. He said that the Lord "is longsuffering toward us, not willing that any should perish but that all should come to repentance" (2 Peter 3:4).

Noah's contemporaries could see the ark as it was being built. They were warned of the coming destruction and yet Jesus said: "They were eating and drinking, marrying and giving in marriage, until the day that Noah entered the ark, and did not know until the flood came and took them all away." Likewise, many of Jesus' generation did not heed the warnings of John the Baptist, Jesus or His apostles, nor did they take into account the signs and wonders performed by Jesus and His disciples. On the day of Pentecost, Peter warned the Jews of "the coming of the great and awesome day of the LORD" (Acts 2:20). In verse 38, he told them to repent and then in verse 40 said: "Be saved from this perverse generation." Despite all of God' gracious warnings, many were caught unaware, both in Noah's day and in the day of the Lord in AD70 when Jerusalem was destroyed.

Let me briefly return to the hypothetical example that I was using above. If I were a truly loving husband and cared for my wife's feelings, I would try to give her any additional information as it became available pertaining to the time of my return. In this way, as the time drew near, she would be ready for my arrival. I believe this is precisely the situation we find with our Lord. It is a fact that while present with them on earth, Jesus told His disciples that He did not know "the hour or the day" of His coming. Likewise, He openly admitted in John 16 that there were things that He could not tell them

24

while He was with them. He also pointed however, to the fact that He would "pray the Father, and He will give you another Helper, that He may abide with you forever-- the Spirit of truth" (John 14:16-17). The Helper would be sent to reveal truth to them.

"I still have many things to say to you, but you cannot bear them now. However, when He, the Spirit of truth, has come, He will guide you into all truth; for He will not speak on His own authority, but whatever He hears He will speak; and He will tell you things to come. He will glorify Me, for He will take of what is Mine and declare it to you. All things that the Father has are Mine. Therefore I said that He will take of Mine and declare it to you" (John 16:12-15).

The Father is the one that Jesus said knew the hour and day that He (Jesus) would return (Matthew 24:36). It was also the Father who was to send the Holy Spirit (John 14:16-17). The Spirit would tell the disciples of "things to come." Note that it is not that the Spirit of truth would simply reveal "truth" in general. Jesus said the Spirit would take what was His (Jesus) and declare it to them. He also said: "All things that the Father has are Mine." The Spirit was to speak whatever He heard, and that would according to Jesus' words, specifically include things that were to come.

Do we as modern readers sometimes forget, or perhaps never even consider, that all the New Testament epistles must be understood in the context of Jesus' teachings in the gospels. These New Testament writers were either taught directly by our Lord, or were in close contact with those who had been. Even the apostle Paul who was not among Jesus' disciples during His earthly ministry, claimed to have received his gospel directly from the Lord, not from any man. "But I make known to you, brethren, that the gospel which was preached by me is not according to man. For I neither received it from man, nor was I taught it, but it came through the revelation of Jesus Christ" (Galatians 1:11-12). Therefore when we read Paul's writings (or for that matter any of the other New Testament writers) we cannot truly understand them apart from Jesus' message in the Gospels. If Jesus spoke of His coming (*'parousia'*) occurring within the timeframe of His generation, then this should help us place Paul's teaching on Christ's coming (*'parousia'*) in its proper setting as well.

In addition we have the opening verse of the Apocalypse. "The Revelation of Jesus Christ, which God gave Him to show His servants--things which must shortly take place" (Revelation 1:1). Note that Jesus is revealing the things that God (Who did know the hour and day) gave Him to show His servants. This completely undoes the objection or concern expressed by many in relation to Matthew 24:36 (also Mark 13:32, Acts 1:7). Notice also that these were things, "which must shortly take place."

Although many modern scholars attribute a late date to the book of Revelation (circa AD95), this was not necessarily the case even as little as 100 years or so ago. There are a growing number who look at the time statements along with other internal biblical evidence and support a pre AD70 dating of this book. It seems highly likely that God the Father was giving further revelation to His servants as the time of the great conflagration rapidly approached. Over and over within this book, are found statements indicating that the events described were to happen soon.

In fact almost identical statements indicating immediate imminence bracket the book itself. "Then he said to me, 'These words are faithful and true.' And the Lord God of the holy prophets sent His angel to

26

show His servants the things which *must* shortly take place" (Revelation 22:6, see also 1:1 above). Note the emphasis. He again states that these things *must* shortly take place! This encompasses all the prophecy between Revelation 1:1 and 22:6, which is essentially the entire prophecy. In Revelation 22:20 Jesus said: "Surely I am coming quickly." This does not mean, as some would say, that when He does come He will come "rapidly." Indeed the NET Bible translates the phrase as follows: "Yes, I am coming soon!"

It is important to note that when God revealed future events to Daniel, he was told to "seal up the vision, for it refers to many days in the future" (Daniel 8:26). In the last chapter of his prophecy Daniel was given further instruction: "Go your way, Daniel, for the words are closed up and sealed till the time of the end (not "the end of time") " (Daniel 12:9). Daniel's prophecy was to be closed up and sealed because at that time "it refers to many days in the future." It would not be fulfilled for hundreds of years.

In dramatic and emphatic contrast, Revelation 22:10 states that the angel said to John: "Do not seal the words of the prophecy of this book, for the time is at hand." How could God express it any more plainly? How can statements like this, and the others already noted, be understood to stretch out for almost 2000 years or perhaps longer? The test of a true prophet of God is not only that the predicted events happen, but also that they occur when predicted. If the prophecy of the book of Revelation did not happen shortly after John wrote it, then it would seem that we must call the one who gave it (Jesus) a false prophet. Whether Revelation was written before or after 70AD, it is clear that John (as it was revealed to him by Jesus) said its prophecies would be fulfilled *soon*. All of the time statements in the book of Revelation are in complete agreement with the teaching of Jesus in the Gospels that all of the things of which He spoke would

27

happen before that 1st century generation passed away. This same principle also characterizes the writings of His disciples in the New Testament epistles.

As Don Preston has frequently noted in his teachings, it was very important to Jesus that His disciples not be deceived as to when He was to come. He described to them a number of signs that must come to pass before the end would come. He also gave notice of several signs that would indicate to them "that it is near at the doors!" Likewise He told them: "Take heed that you not be deceived. For many will come in My name, saying, 'I am He,' and, 'The time has drawn near.' Therefore do not go after them" (Luke 21:8). He did not want them to be deceived into believing that He was coming before His time. He condemned those who would say: "The time has drawn near," before it actually had.

Jesus called for patience, but along with patience there was to be the certainty that at least some in that generation would indeed see the time. "By your patience possess *your* souls. But when *you* see Jerusalem surrounded by armies, then know that its desolation is near" (Luke 21:19-20). His disciples were not to proclaim the nearness of the end until they saw the signs that Jesus said they would see as the time drew near. If Jesus' coming was not near at the time the later epistles were written, then these writers were guilty of precisely the false teaching that Jesus condemned in Luke 21:8. If we hold to the trustworthiness of the scriptures, we must believe that His coming was near at the time of the writing of the later epistles, including the book of Revelation. Paul, Peter, and John clearly affirm that His coming was at hand. Once again please note that if His return was not truly at hand, then these supposedly inspired apostles were guilty of what Jesus had warned against in Luke 21:8.

28

As early as circa AD50, Paul noted that this problem has already arisen in Thessalonica. Some were already proclaiming that the day of Christ had come. "Now, brethren, concerning the coming of our Lord Jesus Christ and our gathering together to Him, we ask you, not to be soon shaken in mind or troubled, either by spirit or by word or by letter, as if from us, as though the day of Christ had come" (2 Thessalonians 2:1-2). His response was to tell them not to let anyone deceive them, and then he reminded them of a specific event that must take place before the day of Christ would come. He did not scold them for being so foolish as to think that the Lord's coming had happened so soon. It wasn't so much a matter of the general timing, but rather a sequence of events that was to take place before Christ would come. All of those events had not taken place as yet, but they *were* expected to occur within the span of that generation. "Let no one deceive you by any means; for that Day will not come unless the falling away comes first, and the man of sin is revealed" (2 Thessalonians 2:3).

It is evident that those in Thessalonica must have been expecting the day of Christ in their generation. Likewise, it is clear that their understanding of the nature of this event was not aligned well at all with that of the large majority of modern Christians. If the day of the Lord (Christ) was truly expected to be a literal earth burning, time ending event, then how could a reasonable person be convinced that it had already occurred? This question seems to somehow evade the minds of most believers today (For a much more detailed discussion of this question, see Don Preston's book *How Is This Possible?*).

Another issue that needs to be seriously considered flows directly from this problem that Paul encountered with the Thessalonians. It is similar in principle to a problem that Paul mentioned in writing to Timothy: "But shun profane and idle babblings, for they will increase

29

to more ungodliness. And their message will spread like cancer. Hymenaeus and Philetus are of this sort, who have strayed concerning the truth, saying that the resurrection is already past; and they overthrow the faith of some" (2 Timothy 2:16-18).

In one instance, false teachers had come in and convinced some in Thessalonica that Christ had already come. In the other situation, Hymenaeus and Philetus had apparently persuaded some in Ephesus that the resurrection was past (Preston has another book titled *The Hymenaean Heresy - Reverse The Charges*, which gives a detailed analysis of this very important issue).

A serious question must be asked: if modern concepts of the second coming and the resurrection are correct, then how could anyone possibly convince others that these two events were already past? It would have been simple to disprove either claim by pointing to the physical evidence readily visible to everyone. Certainly no one's faith would be overthrown by such an obviously erroneous assertion. Isn't this really the crux of the problem?

The reason preterists are so vehemently opposed in many Christian circles is because the predominant concept of the Second Coming and the resurrection cannot allow for a past fulfillment. However, the concept of the nature of these events held by at least some 1st century Christians, allowed them to be convinced that these events had already taken place. Both of these passages must give us serious reason to pause and perhaps re-evaluate the dominant ideas regarding the nature of Christ's Second Coming and the closely linked resurrection of the dead. Perhaps the "literal" interpretations and expectations commonly put forth are not as "unchallengeable" as so many would have us believe.

30

The method of Jesus in His earthly ministry was to reinforce the teaching that His coming would be within the lifetime of some of His disciples within their generation. We generally do not find statements in the gospels that indicate a sense of *immediate* imminence as is found in much of the later apostolic writings. He gave them signs to look for that would tell them when the time was near, but gave them no indication that His coming was as yet "at the door." That was to be a message presented as the end of that generation approached.

The early writings of Paul bear a similar approach. [An interesting exercise to confirm this pattern would be for the reader to comb the New Testament scriptures for statements related to "the end" and as best as possible, place them in chronological order. The reader can then see as my friend Jim Wade noted: "the crescendo of imminence as AD 70 approaches."] In some of the statements found in his earlier letters to the Thessalonians and the Corinthians, Paul indicated that although some may die, or most likely would die, before the coming of the Lord, others of them would still be alive. To the Thessalonians he said: "For this we say to you by the word of the Lord, that we who are alive and remain until the coming of the Lord will by no means precede those who are asleep," and then "we who are alive and remain shall be caught up together with them in the clouds to meet the Lord in the air" (1 Thessalonians 4:15, 17).

These statements were made to 1st century Christians. If he did not share the expectation that all these things would occur within that contemporary generation, Paul could easily have made his point by saying, "Whoever is alive when He comes will be caught up in the air." That would have left it open ended and indefinite, but that is not what he said.

31

Paul included himself among that group of contemporary Christians out of whom his expectation was that some would be alive when the Lord came. Note the certainty with which Paul wrote. It was not speculation, or just a mere hope. He was certain that some to whom he was writing would be alive at Christ's coming. There was no maybe in these statements. He wasn't expecting the Lord's return immediately, but had a definite expectation that His return would be within the lifetime of some of his contemporaries.

To those at Corinth he said, "Behold, I tell you a mystery: We shall not all sleep, but we shall all be changed" (1 Corinthians 15:51). In other words, he was telling them that although it may be some time before the Lord would come, at least some of them would definitely be alive at that great day. Just as Jesus had said, it would be within that generation. Paul made this demonstrably clear when he said, "we shall not all sleep." It is clear that his use of "sleep" in this context was in reference to physical death. Paul was dealing with the specific issue of the coming of Christ and was not stating categorically that some would never die (sleep), but rather that some would not die before that momentous event occurred.

To conclude this chapter, let me share an anecdote that highlights what I perceive to be a significant problem with futurist eschatology. Recently as my wife and I were taking our, at the time 6 year old, grandson to rendezvous with his parents, he was continually asking, as children typically do, how long before we would reach our destination. About 2 miles from the point we were to meet, he asked his question once again. My wife turned and replied that we would be there soon. His frustrated response was classic (at least in my mind): "Soon is forever!" Certainly futurist understand the normal meaning of soon, but when one hears teachers quoting biblical passages that speak of "soon to happen" events and then applying them to our day and age, it appears that they elasticize the meaning far beyond reason and that perhaps in their minds there is at least a sense in which "soon is forever".

"This Generation": Contemporary or Not?

The correct understanding of "this generation" in Matthew 24:34 has been a source of considerable disagreement in recent years and in reality for much of the history of the church. Sometime ago I encountered a webpage titled *Why Partial Preterism is Wrong* that purports to show why partial preterism (which as noted above is the belief that much prophecy was indeed fulfilled in A.D.70, but that Christ will still come again in the future) is incorrect in its understanding of fulfilled prophecy. Much of the author's argument is centered around this verse. The writer (who does not identify himself or provide any means to respond to him) early on writes off Full Preterism by stating,

> "Full preterism is an extremely strange view that everything in the entire Book of Revelation was fulfilled prior to 70 A.D., including a symbolic rapture of the saints, the Antichrist, Babylon in Revelation etc. This is so far from the truth that very few believe it."

As has already been noted, many would agree that Full Preterism is "an extremely strange view" because it is dramatically different, at least in its conclusions, from all of the "most popular" eschatological views. It is interesting however, that proponents of Full Preterism, if they pick and choose can readily find support from various different "orthodox" scholars for their interpretation of virtually every critical eschatological passage of scripture that they address. That is certainly not to say that these "orthodox" scholars agree with the ultimate conclusions reached by the Full Preterist. It does indicate, however, that Full Preterism is perhaps not so "strange" as some believe it to be. Is it strange that some students of the Bible would choose to take

34

seriously the words of Revelation 22:10 where the angel says to John, "Do not seal the words of the prophecy of this book, for the time is as hand?" Is it strange that some would take Jesus at His word as He closes His revelation to John by saying, "Surely I am coming quickly"? ("Yes, I am coming soon" NET Bible on-line [Note that the NET translation is a product associated with Dallas Theological Seminary which does not tend towards a preterist understanding of the book of Revelation]).

The writer just mentioned proceeds by providing a long list of "end time" events and then states what he believes to be the "rationale for preterism." That "rationale" is that partial preterists believe all these events happened before 70 A.D., because of three Bible verses. In Mt 24:34; Mk 13:30; and Lk 21:32 Jesus said that *this generation* will not pass away until *all* these things have happened.

Statements such as this are a source of extreme frustration for me, and I'm sure for others who hold to fulfilled eschatology. It is obvious that this person either has not thoroughly studied the position that he is critiquing, or else he is being disingenuous. If he has thoroughly studied the preterist teachings he knows full well that there are a multitude of verses that point to the 1st century imminence of the end, rather than just the three he referenced. These three verses are indeed very powerful statements that support the preterist position, and I believe they demand serious consideration by any Bible student. They do say, as the author notes that "this generation" will not pass away until *all* these things take place. It is interesting to see how some try to show how "this generation" really means some other generation and that "all" really only means some. Nevertheless, there are a multitude of other passages that provide overwhelming support for the time indicators found in these three verses.

John MacArthur also identifies Matthew 24:34 as a key verse upon which preterists hang their hat. He says, "Preterist, of course, place much stress on this verse. They insist it guarantees that the generation alive during Jesus' time would be the same generation to see the complete fulfillment of all these signs, and they treat it as the key that unlocks the meaning of the Olivet Discourse" (p.133).

It is interesting that MacArthur agrees with the author of the article cited above and yet includes an appendix titled *The Imminent Return of the Redeemer*, which is a long excerpt (p.197 - 215 in MacArthur's book) from a book titled *The Redeemer's Return* by A.W. Pink in which Pink goes to great lengths to show that throughout the New Testament is found language pointing to an imminent return of Christ. The reason MacArthur includes this material is because of the "explanations" that Pink gives to answer the question "Why is it that our Lord has tarried till now?" Although Pink's answers are supportive of and very similar to the "answers" to the same question that MacArthur gives earlier in the book, Pink's answers are exposed by the same critiques offered here and in works by many other preterist authors.

MacArthur goes on to say that, "the reasonable mind quickly sees the folly of having to allegorize so many passages of Scripture just for the sake of interpreting one verse (v.34) with such rigid literalism. It is simply not necessary to insist that Christ meant that all the Olivet Discourse signs must be fulfilled in that current generation" (p.133). Even here MacArthur implicitly acknowledges that the correct understanding of "this generation" refers to that current 1st century generation, and apparently his insistence on interpreting the signs, many of which are expressed in metaphoric (not allegorical) language, with "rigid literalism" causes him to reject the force of the plain, straightforward language of Matthew 24:34. It would appear therefore, that in his mind it is proper to interpret the signs with rigid literalism but not the time statements despite the use of language in these passages that would seem to dictate the opposite approach. This will be addressed in more depth later.

What MacArthur and others with similar views choose to do is essentially re-write what Matthew said that Jesus said. MacArthur says, "the signs are a package. When they are truly fulfilled, they will be fulfilled all at once. That seems to be the gist of this parable, as well as the comment that follows it. Therefore, the most reasonable interpretation of verse 34 is this: Christ is saying that the generation alive when the true labor pains begin will be the same generation that sees the delivery. These things, when they happen, will not stretch out across generations" (p.133). So what MacArthur is trying to tell his readers is that Jesus did not really mean what His words most obviously (literally) seemed to say. He must therefore re-interpret Jesus' words (this is precisely what he does) so that they fit his paradigm. The problem is that his "reasonable" interpretation is not what Jesus plainly stated according to the biblical text. Read virtually any Bible translation and you will not find Jesus saying in any of them what MacArthur says He means.

Turning back to the article, this writer calls into question the way preterist understand *generation* in these three verses. He correctly states that the Greek word *genea* can be understood in several different senses. As far as I can tell however, there is no evidence in the Greek lexicons that *genea* may legitimately be understood and translated as "race." There is a closely related Greek word that may be defined as, "kindred, offspring, or family." That word is *genos*, but that is not the word used in the passages under discussion.

There are a number of factors that must be taken into account in determining precisely what sense is appropriate for each usage. Obviously the immediate context is most critical, but we would also want to examine if possible, how the particular writer or speaker uses this word in other passages. Again, if possible we should seek to let scripture interpret scripture, not only by looking at other passages that use the same word, but other passages that deal with the same issue or context.

This writer has chosen to ignore other statements that Jesus made in which He spoke of His imminent return without using the Greek word *genea*. I refer the reader to Matthew 10:23, 16:27-28, and 26:64 in which Jesus clearly stated that His coming would occur before all of those living at that time had died.

One of the primary definitions of *genea* is "the whole multitude of men living at the same time." Although Jesus does not use the word *genea* in the three passages listed immediately above, His statements carry the same sense as we commonly understand generation today and as is reflected in the definition above. The fact that Jesus stated in other passages that He would come before all of His contemporaries died should significantly impact our understanding of the sense in which He used the word *genea*.

Matthew 23 is a crucial passage that must be considered when attempting to understand what Jesus intended by the use of the phrase "this generation" in Matthew 24:34 (as well as the parallel passages of Mark 13:30 and Luke 21:32). In Matthew chapter 23, Jesus spoke of and to a specific group of people: the scribes and Pharisees. Over and over again Jesus castigated the scribes and Pharisees, calling them hypocrites and leveling a litany of charges against them. In verses 31-36 He made it plain that He was speaking to a group of then living people.

"Therefore you are witnesses against yourselves that you are sons of those who murdered the prophets. Fill up, then, the measure of your fathers' guilt. Serpents, brood of vipers! How can you escape the condemnation of hell? Therefore, indeed, I send you prophets, wise men, and scribes: some of them you will kill and crucify, and some of them you will scourge in your synagogues and persecute from city to city, that on you may come all the righteous blood shed on the earth, from the blood of righteous Abel to the blood of Zechariah, son of Berechiah, whom you murdered between the temple and the altar. Assuredly, I say to you, all these things will come upon this generation" (Matthew 24:31-36).

There was a distinction made between the group to whom He was actually speaking and their fathers, and yet Jesus made it plain that the present group would be held responsible for "all the righteous blood shed on the earth, from the blood of righteous Abel to the blood of Zechariah." In verse 30, Jesus said the scribes and Pharisees have said: "If we had lived in the days of our fathers, we would not have been partakers with them in the blood of the prophets." Jesus emphatically denied their claim by saying: "I send *you* prophets, wise men, and scribes: some of them *you* will kill and crucify (this obviously would include Jesus), and some of them *you* will scourge in *your* synagogues and persecute from city to city." He was speaking directly to a specific group of people who were alive to hear His words, and their future actions would confirm Jesus' accusations against them. The New Testament record verifies that they did indeed treat His disciples as Jesus predicted.

39

It is undeniable that Jesus was pointing to a coming climax that would be as a result of all the guilt that had built up throughout the many generations of those that had persecuted and murdered the righteous. According to the words of Jesus, those living at that time were going to fill up "the measure of their father's guilt." This was the same "brood of vipers" to whom John the Baptist warned of the wrath that was "about to come" (Greek word *mello*: "to be on the point of doing or suffering something"). It seems probable that when Jesus said: "All these things will come upon this generation," He was referring either to that specific group of scribes and Pharisees (another definition of *genea* is "a group of men very much like each other in endowments, pursuits, and character especially in a bad sense, a perverse nation"), or to the Jews as a "nation" living at that time. This would be the "terminal generation" in the sense that "all these things will come upon" them. Surely this is the sense in which we should understand Jesus' use of the phrase in Matthew 24:34 as well. While commentators almost universally accept Jesus' use of generation in Matthew 23 as referring to people contemporary to Him, many of the same will modify their understanding and deny its contemporary character in chapter 24, without any apparent textual justification for making a distinction between the two passages.

Jesus spoke of "this generation" in a number of other passages. These should help the student see how He typically used this word and how He intended it to be understood by His disciples. He spoke of "an evil and adulterous generation," of a "wicked generation," a "wicked and adulterous generation," a "faithless and perverse generation," and an "adulterous and sinful generation," each time speaking directly to a group of His contemporaries. This was the generation that would fill up the measure of their father's guilt (Matthew 23:32).

In Matthew 12, a group of the scribes and Pharisees came to Jesus saying, "We want to see a sign from You." In His response to their request, He called them an "evil and adulterous generation" and proceeded to condemn those who were alive at that time and who had heard His message but had not believed. He told them: "The men of Nineveh will rise up in the judgment with this generation and condemn it" (Matthew 12:41) because the Ninevites had believed Jonah's message. He also said: "The queen of the South will rise up in the judgment with this generation and condemn it" (Matthew 12:42) because she came to hear the wisdom of Solomon. "This generation" was undoubtedly the contemporary group (perhaps inclusive of those in Jerusalem and Judea in general) who had heard John and then Jesus preach about the coming kingdom, and was directed specifically at those who had not believed or repented.

Jesus' "this generation" was the only people to whom the message had been directly given by John, Jesus and His disciples. It was not a reference to a whole race of people inclusive of their whole history. Throughout the gospels Jesus specifically addressed His contemporary Jewish "brethren" and He closed that little exchange in Matthew 12 by emphasizing the extremely wicked nature of many of that present "wicked generation."

Although John does not use the Greek word *genea* in any of his writings, there is a passage that is relevant to the discussion and that should help give a clearer understanding of some of these other passages. John 4:48 expresses condemnation of those seeking a sign, that is similar to what is found in the synoptic gospels when Jesus condemned "this generation." "Unless you people see signs and wonders, you will by no means believe" (NKJV). Jesus' use of the phrase "you people" is directly analogous to the phrase "this generation" used in the other gospels. Again it is obvious that He was speaking directly to a contemporary group of people and not a particular "race."

Finally, it should be noted how Matthew used the word *genea* in the writing of his gospel when not specifically quoting Jesus. In the first chapter of his gospel, Matthew presented the genealogy of our Lord. Upon completion He made this concluding statement: "So all the generations from Abraham to David are fourteen generations, from David until the captivity in Babylon are fourteen generations, and from the captivity in Babylon until the Christ are fourteen generations" (Matthew 1:17). Surely his use here is referring to individuals belonging to successive groups of people living together at the same time. Although not absolutely conclusive or definitive, this usage should re-enforce the sense of "men living together at the same time" as the primary meaning of the word *genea* in Matthew's writing. This should certainly be taken into consideration when attempting to determine the correct understanding of "this generation" in Matthew 24:34.

Whether Jesus was delimiting His use of generation to the contemporary group of scribes and Pharisees, or to all of the contemporary Jews does not impact the sense of imminence in relation to all of His contemporaries. If He told the then living "generation" of scribes and Pharisees that "on you may come all the righteous blood shed on the earth," it would still result in "all these things" happening within the lifetime of the broader "generation" alive in Jesus' day.

In order to be sure to fairly address this issue, the Old Testament must at least be mentioned. There are 129 passages in the New King James Version that translate the Hebrew word *dowr* as generation (in its singular and plural forms). In the vast majority of them the meaning undoubtedly refers to "those living during a period." Two passages from Deuteronomy 32 (verses 5 and 20), to which Jesus and the New Testament writers allude when addressing their contemporaries, are referring to a specific group of people in the last days of Israel.

The writer to the Hebrews also gives insight into the Biblical meaning of generation. In chapter 3, he quoted Psalm 95:8-11, which dealt with God's displeasure with the wilderness generation that He had delivered from Egyptian captivity. He made it obvious when he said that they "saw My works forty years," that He was referring to a group of people living together at the same time. This usage directly parallels Jesus' use of generation throughout His ministry. His frustration and anger with them because of their unbelief, was evident on numerous occasions. Just as God had dealt with a specific generation living together at the same time in the exodus from Egypt, so Jesus was also passing judgment on a specific generation. They had seen His miracles and heard His message, and yet many had not believed that He was the Son of God.

In the vast majority of cases in the entire Bible, there are no contextual reasons to understand generation as anything other than a group of people living at the same time. It would seem that it should require clear and compelling contextual justification in order to veer from the overwhelmingly predominant usage of this word found throughout the scriptures. It would also appear that the only reason to even consider a different meaning stems from preconceived notions based on eschatological systems that cannot deal effectively with the proper understanding.

In a debate held in October of 2002 between futurists Kevin Hartley and Gary George, and preterists Ed Stevens and Don Preston, Hartley lashed out at the veracity of the testimony of Josephus' description of the destruction of Jerusalem circa AD70. In the quote below it can be seen that he lends no credence to the historical account of this destruction as in any way a fulfillment of Jesus' Olivet Discourse. In his mind, those prophesies could have been just as easily fulfilled, or not, in numerous other historical events such as the day of Constantine or the sixteenth century Reformation.

"Several other events of the age of Christendom could be equated with the Parousia. The day of Constantine and era, the sixteenth century Reformation. If I was to sit down and read prophetic language and to simply apply it to the events of history through several times in history, I could come to the same conclusions that Josephus came to, which is that the prophetic language can be applied to almost any circumstance. So who's to say that Josephus and what he wrote was accurate?"

Once again, if we detach Jesus' words from their primary context regarding the audience to whom He was speaking, there may be at least enough in Hartley's statement to give us cause to momentarily reconsider our position. However, as soon as we turn back to the actual text and context of that particular passage, it appears quite certain that there is no justification for the reasoning behind his statement.

This is an issue of immense importance and I will repeat a statement I made in an earlier work regarding the book of Revelation. The principle is equally relevant to the study of all the New Testament documents. "If the one investigating this revelation were to take these words seriously, it would give him/her a specific and limited context

44

in which to begin and carry out his investigation. It would simplify the search for truth by placing upon it a specific time constraint. It would eliminate much of the varied and farfetched speculations commonly found in today's religious writings. By honoring these time parameters the searcher would be able to confine his studies to events contemporaneous to the writing of the book. In my view, this is the key hermeneutic that should guide any study of this book." (*Who Was The Mother of Harlots?*, 2012, p.20-21.)

It is of particular interest to me that many critics decry the emphasis placed by the full preterist on the time statements. Although many of these critics fully recognize and embrace many of the time statements, especially when they support their particular positions, yet when the full preterist look to fall back on these numerous New Testament statements in order to ground their understanding of certain passages within a specific scripturally based context, these critics throw up their hands in exasperation as if trying to free themselves from the contextual and temporal shackles that these time statements would clearly seem to place upon them. Without the limitations and restrictions that these statements afford, ignoring them or explaining them away frees the student to explore unconstrained and speculate about possibilities that seem to be outside the bounds of what the scriptures would legitimately allow.

Many of these time statements are as direct and straightforward as any statements found within the Bible, but some apparently speculate that since there are other biblical statements that because of the nature of their poetic, metaphoric, figurative or apocalyptic language, are not always to be taken at face value, perhaps we cannot really be certain that we properly understand the true meaning of these prosaic times statements. Can we really be sure that we can take them at face value? Let me just ask the reader, if we cannot take what seem

45

to be the clearest and most straightforward statements found in the scriptures, such as the following - "And he said to me, 'Do not seal the words of the prophecy of this book, for the time is at hand'" (Revelation 22:10) – at face value, how can we be confident that our reading and understanding of any passage is correct?

It might reasonably be said that the time statements are like a map that restricts our exploration and keeps us focused within the proper area to be studied. Although we may have the whole world before us to explore and have been given some localized instructions to guide our search, if we have not been given a map that points us to the proper location to begin, as well as the area within which to restrict our search, we are highly unlikely to ultimately arrive at the proper destination.

That is why preterists cling so tightly to these clear and unambiguous statements found throughout the New Testament. They may seem restrictive to some, but they will keep us on target if allowed to consistently to be our guide. Surely they have been ignored by a great many down through the history of the church, but it is not too late to break from this course which has led to such tremendous confusion for hundreds of years now.

Matthew 24:3 said that "the disciples came to Him privately." There can be no doubt then that when in verse 4 Matthew said: "Jesus answered and said to them" that the *them* referred to are His disciples. As He continued through this discourse it should also be self evident that the *you* to whom He directed His comments were His disciples. Fifteen times between verses 4 and 34, we find these personal pronouns explicitly directed to his disciples. All throughout this passage, Jesus was clearly speaking directly to His disciples and telling them about things that they would see and experience.

In verses 4-8, Jesus specifically warned these disciples not to be deceived by false christs. He told them that *they* would hear of wars and rumors of wars. This is one of the signs that many today tells us are to take place in some "last days" period in our own day or some time yet future to us. It is perfectly clear however, that Jesus was telling the men hearing His words in the 1st century that these things would happen in their lifetime. He told them that "nation will rise against nation, and kingdom against kingdom. And there will be famines, pestilences, and earthquakes in various places" (v.7). Again, these are things that modern day prophesy "experts" say are happening now or must happen in our future. The problem is that Jesus stated as plainly as possible that His disciples (those in His presence) would see these things. He had told them in verse 6 that they would "hear of wars and rumors of wars." They were not to be troubled when they heard of those things because they must come to pass, "but the end is not yet." The end of what? His disciples had just asked Him about the end of the age, so that must certainly be what He was referring to here. Although seldom noted, this comment is very important to our understanding of the disciple's expectations.

Many teach that the disciples were expecting an end of the "world" that would result in the destruction of the physical creation. They point to passages such as 2 Peter 3, 1 Thessalonians 5, and 2 Thessalonians 1, which spoke of the destruction of heaven and earth, sudden destruction, and flaming fire and everlasting destruction. These they see as parallel to Matthew 24. Jesus however, knew that when the disciples heard of wars and rumors of war, they would believe that the end of the age was upon them. It is apparent that they did not associate the end of the age with cosmic destruction; rather they expected war to be evidence of the approaching end of the age. No doubt Jesus said that wars and rumors of war did not mean that the

47

end was at hand, but they were indeed the beginning of the sorrows that were associated with the end. The point is that in the context of the coming end of the age, the disciples expected it to be associated with human warfare and Jesus did nothing to dissuade them of this notion.

In verse 9, He told them that after *they* saw these things then "they will deliver *you* up to tribulation and kill *you,* and *you* will be hated by all nations for My name's sake." The Revised English Bible translation of verses 9 and 10 makes it particularly clear that Jesus is describing a sequence of events. "*You* will then be handed over for punishment and execution; all nations will hate *you* for *your* allegiance to me. *At that time* many will fall from their faith; they will betray one another and hate one another." Verses 9 and 10 describe things that Jesus said would happen to His 1st century disciples after they witnessed the things described in verses 4-8.

"Therefore when you see the 'abomination of desolation,' spoken of by Daniel the prophet, standing in the holy place" (whoever reads, let him understand), "then let those who are in Judea flee to the mountains. Let him who is on the housetop not go down to take anything out of his house. And let him who is in the field not go back to get his clothes. But woe to those who are pregnant and to those who are nursing babies in those days! And pray that your flight may not be in winter or on the Sabbath. For then there will be great tribulation, such as has not been since the beginning of the world until this time, no, nor ever shall be. And unless those days were shortened, no flesh would be saved; but for the elect's sake those days will be shortened. 'Then if anyone says to you, 'Look, here is the Christ!' or 'There!' do not believe it. For false christs and false prophets will rise and show great signs

48

and wonders to deceive, if possible, even the elect. See, I have told you beforehand'" (Matthew 24:15-25).

As can be seen above, Jesus continued to tell those present before Him of things that they would see and experience. He was warning them so that they would not be deceived into thinking that He had come before it was time. He said, "see, I have told *you* beforehand" (v.25). His expectation was that His disciples would be confronted with these temptations. In verse 26, He said: "Therefore if they say to *you* (His 1st century disciples)." His disciples alive in the 1st century would be the ones to hear these claims, not people living two thousand years or more in the future.

In Verses 29 through 31, Jesus described events that would take place immediately prior to His coming. He once again made it explicitly plain that it was His 1st century disciples who would see these signs. In verse 33, He said: "So you (His 1st century disciples) *also, when you* (His 1st century disciples) see all these things, know that it is near - at the doors." How could Jesus make it any more clear that His 1st century disciples were going to see "all these things"? The text explicitly states that according to Jesus, His 1st century disciples would see "all these things" that He had laid out before them in the preceding verses.

In case they didn't believe or understand what He was saying, Jesus followed with a statement that has caused great difficulty in the minds of many for much of the last almost two thousand years. In the September 1996 volume of the Journal of the Evangelical Theological Society, Neil D. Nelson wrote an article entitled *"This Generation" In Matthew 24:34: A Literary Critical Perspective*. His first sentence states the following: "The expression *he genea haute* ("this generation") in the Olivet discourse remains what Joseph A.

49

Fitzmyer has termed 'the most difficult phrase to interpret in this complicated eschatological discourse.'"

Taken in its proper context, however, it seems quite plain what Jesus was doing and saying. The difficulty is in trying to reconcile this important passage with any non preterist approach to eschatology. He was simply reasserting and reinforcing His previous statement (verse 33). He said, "Assuredly, I say to you." He was speaking directly to His 1st century disciples. He told them "this generation will by no means pass away until all these things take place." It is really very clear if we will only take it for what it says and understand to whom Jesus was speaking.

In verse 36 of chapter 24, Jesus made another statement that has needlessly troubled and confused many down through the years. He said, "of that day and hour no one knows." How many times have I heard or read men interpret this statement as indicating that no one can have any idea whatsoever when that day would come? This despite the fact that in verse 33 Jesus said His disciples would "see all these things," and in verse 34, He said that "these things" would take place before that generation passed away. There is a major difference between knowing the precise day and hour (which is what, per Jesus, no one knew) something is to happen, versus knowing the general timeframe in which it is to take place. Jesus gave them (His 1st century disciples) a general timeframe, as well as signs that would alert them (His 1st century disciples) when the time was at hand. Verse 36 in no way negates Jesus' statements in verses 33 and 34. It only served to emphasize the need for them (His 1st century disciples) to be ever vigilant and alert, to be aware of what was happening in the world around them. This is the exclusive emphasis of Jesus' teaching in the remaining verses of chapter 24 and the beginning verses of chapter 25.

In 24:42 He said: "*Watch* therefore, for *you* (His 1st century disciples) do not know what hour your Lord is coming." In verse 44 He said: "Therefore *you* (His 1st century disciples) also be ready, for the Son of Man is coming at an hour *you* (His 1st century disciples) do not expect." He told two parables that strongly emphasize the need for *them* to be vigilant and ever watchful. He condemned the evil servant who said in his heart "my master is delaying his coming" (24:48).

In Matthew 25:1-13, Jesus told the parable of the wise and foolish virgins, again stressing the importance of being ready when the "bridegroom" came. One last time, He told His 1st century disciples to "watch therefore, for you (His 1st century disciples) know neither the day nor the hour in which the Son of Man is coming" (v.13). They could not know the day or hour, but they did know that their precious Lord had told them that "there were some standing here who shall not taste death till they see the Son of Man coming in His Kingdom" (Matthew 10:23). They knew that based upon what Jesus had told them, their contemporary generation would not pass away until all these things happened!

Therefore, if we allow the text to guide us, we cannot put these things three hundred, fifteen hundred or even two thousand or more years down the road. Jesus was clear that His 1st century disciples would see His coming. We are not dependent upon the testimony of Josephus or any other historian. They simply corroborate what Jesus said would happen and yet aside from their testimony, we take Him at His word and choose to walk by faith, trusting that His words are true - allowing His statements to define and guide our interpretation.

Luke 21 is parallel to Matthew 24. Once again it is important that we look at Luke's account in order to fully understand what is taught by

51

Matthew. Just as Matthew does, Luke listed a number of signs that would signify the soon coming of the Son of Man. In verse 32 he made the same assertion regarding "this generation" not passing away until "all things" take place as was made in Matthew 24:34. A few verses later, Luke recorded Jesus' statement warning His 1st century disciples to be watchful and always praying. "Watch therefore, and pray always that *you* may be counted worthy to escape all these things that will come to pass, and to stand before the Son of Man" (v.36).

In this translation (NKJ) there is nothing that really demands an expectation of imminence other than the fact that Jesus is speaking directly to His 1st century disciples with the obvious implication that some of them would be alive when "these things" come to pass. If we look at the Greek text, as well as several other standard translations, we find that this verse is a powerful confirmation that Jesus' reference to 'this generation" was indeed an explicit reference to those living in His day. The Greek word *mello* is found in this sentence and is translated in the NKJ as "will come." This word properly translated, imparts a definite sense of imminence as is reflected in the phrase "about to" in the translations of this verse listed below.

"But keep on the alert at all times, praying that you may have strength to escape all these things that are *about to* take place, and to stand before the Son of Man" (Luke 21:36, New American Standard Bible).

"Be always on the watch, and pray that you may be able to escape all that *is about* to happen, and that you may be able to stand before the Son of Man" (Luke 21:36, New International Version).

"Watch ye, then, in every season, praying that ye may be accounted worthy to escape all these things that are *about to* come to pass, and to stand before the Son of Man'" (Luke 21:36, Young's Literal Translation).

Many other standard translations (such as the KJV, NKV, and RSV among others) seem reluctant to apply this established meaning in the many other places where *mello* is found in the Greek text. The imminence associated with this word is not seriously questioned in the standard Greek lexicons. When one goes through the New Testament and identifies where *mello* is found and then applies wording reflecting the proper emphasis on imminence, it dramatically changes the temporal meaning of many passages.

We will look at a few verses and see how significant the use of this proper emphasis on eminence can be on some very crucial New Testament texts. In the verses listed below (NKJ), I have emphasized the phrases translated from the word *mello* and have inserted in parentheses what I feel is a more appropriate rendering of the meaning of this word.

"Far above all principality and power and might and dominion, and every name that is named, not only in this age but also in that which is to come (is about to come)" (Ephesians 1:21).

"Because He has appointed a day on which He will judge (is about to judge) the world in righteousness by the Man whom

He has ordained. He has given assurance of this to all by raising Him from the dead" (Acts 17:31).

Young's Literal Translation:[31] 'Because He did set a day in which He is about to judge the world in righteousness, by a man whom He did ordain, having given assurance to all, having raised him out of the dead.'

"I have hope in God, which they themselves also accept, that there will be (is about to be) a resurrection of the dead, both of the just and the unjust" (Acts 24:15).

Young's Literal Translation:[15] "Having hope toward God, which they themselves also wait for, (that) there is about to be a rising again of the dead, both of righteous and unrighteous."

Later in Acts 24, there is another verse where the proper interpretation of mello clarifies what can otherwise be a challenging verse. "Now as he reasoned about righteousness, self-control, and the judgment to come (about to come), Felix was afraid and answered, 'Go away for now; when I have a convenient time I will call for you'" (Acts 24:25). Have you ever wondered why Felix was afraid? If he understood Paul to say that the judgment was *about to come*, then it is quite easy and reasonable to see why he may have been shaken by Paul's words.

Is it valid to insert this meaning into these verses where it is not emphasized? I obviously think that it is, especially when it is acknowledged that the *translation* of the Greek text is not inspired. Considering all of the other passages we have examined that point to an imminent return of Christ, there are no compelling contextual or grammatical reasons not to translate *mello* (with the infinitive) in such a way as to allow its primary meaning to be properly expressed.

If we once again search through the New Testament, we would find that there are many instances where the translators used the phrase "about to", or an equivalent phrase clearly emphasizing imminence, when translating *mello*. Why should this not be the case in the verses cited above? In the book of Acts alone we find this situation in a number of passages. A brief look at the NKJ and the NASB versions will give ample evidence of this.

"Who, seeing Peter and John *about to go* into the temple, asked for alms" (Acts 3:3 NKJ).

"And when Paul was *about to* open his mouth" (Acts 18:14 NKJ).

"And when the Jews plotted against him as he *was about to* sail to Syria" (Acts 20:3 NKJ).

"Then as Paul *was about to* be led into the barracks" (Acts 21:37 NKJ).

"Then immediately those who *were about to* examine him withdrew from him" (Acts 22:29 NKJ).

"Consider myself fortunate, King Agrippa, that I am *about to* make my defense before you today" (26:2 NASB).

55

"Until the day *was about to* dawn, Paul was encouraging them all to take some food" (Acts 27:33 NASB).

"But they were expecting that he was *about to* swell up or suddenly fall down dead" (Acts 28:6 NASB).

It is likely that most Christians are not even aware that there is any controversy regarding interpretation of this Greek word. However, it can have a tremendous impact on the message expressed in many important passages. Many commentators recognize and understand the proper or primary meaning of *mello*, but for whatever reason have chosen to accept many of these translations as they stand. Certainly translating passages as I have suggested above would require theologians to seriously reconsider many long held beliefs. Several passages in the book of Hebrews would be significantly impacted if translated according to this primary meaning of *mello*. "But Christ came as High Priest of the good things to come (*about to come*)" (Hebrew 9:11).

The same applies to these other verses from Hebrews: 1:14, 2:5, 6:5, 10:1, 13:14. Although there are many more passages that could be cited, let me conclude with one from Romans. In Romans 8:18 Paul said, "For I consider that the sufferings of this present time are not worthy to be compared with the glory *which shall be* revealed in us" (NKJ). Young's Literal Translation presents this verse as follows: "For I reckon that the sufferings of the present time [are] not worthy [to be compared] with the glory *about to be* revealed in us." Each of these verses if properly translated, would present a sense of imminence that is not commonly recognized, but which accurately reflects and agrees with numerous other passages found throughout the New Testament

56

As we continue looking at Jesus' discourse in Matthew 24-25, note that some have taken verse 19 of chapter 25 (see also 25:5: "But while the bridegroom was delayed") as an indication that, or as justification for the belief that the Lord's coming will not be until many, many, years (meaning thousands of years) into the future. After all they say, it says: *"after a long time the lord of those servants came."* I have heard this argument used on a number of occasions. If one were to take this statement out of its first century human context, perhaps a gap of two thousand years could be justified. The problem however, is that unless we can be convinced that the servants in this parable lived at least two thousand years, this assertion falls apart.

Not surprisingly, this parable fits in perfectly with all that Jesus had told His disciples in chapter 24, as well as in the preceding verses of chapter 25. In this parable, it is undeniable that the servants were alive when their lord departed on his trip to a far country (just as Jesus' disciples were alive when He ascended to heaven). Likewise, it is undeniable that they were still alive when he returned. Therefore the "long time" cannot be stretched into thousands of years, but it fits perfectly within the framework of a biblical generation.

From a human perspective (which is precisely the perspective from which the story is told), if I had to be separated from a loved one for forty years or so, in my mind that would certainly qualify as a very long time in the context of my lifetime. I think this is an important concept that must be addressed. Those who continue to insist that the reason we cannot take the biblical time statements at face value is because God sees time differently than we do, need to explain why Jesus spoke his parables in obviously human terms. He spoke in parables, at least in part, in order that His disciples might more clearly understand the things about which He spoke. He used images that they would clearly understand, and it would have been deceptive of Him to use them as He did if He did not intend them to be understood on a human level and context.

If we assume, for the sake of argument, that Jesus ascended to heaven in 30AD and returned in 70AD, then it would be safe to say that in the minds of His disciples who were still alive at His coming, He had been absent a "long time." At the time Peter wrote his second epistle, scoffers (who had obviously heard or been taught that Christ's coming was to be soon) were apparently already claiming that it had been a "long time" and that the "bridegroom was delayed." They were saying, "Where is the promise of His coming?" (2 Peter 3:4). They were impatient and denying the truth of Christ's soon coming because in their 1st century minds, it had already been a long time. If Jesus did in fact come in 70AD, then it is indisputable that He would have fully satisfied the language He had used when He told His 1st century disciples that all these things (including the coming of the Son of Man) would happen before His contemporary generation passed away.

The same principle applies to the parable of the virgins in v.1-13. Although the "bridegroom was delayed" (v.5), his return was, according to the clear words of this parable (v.10), still to be within the lifetime of the virgins. This is precisely the point, and it is the reason that Jesus concluded with this warning to His disciples: "Watch therefore, for you know neither the day nor the hour in which the Son of Man is coming" (v.13). Some of them would be alive and they were to faithfully watch for the signs that Jesus had given them.

It is apparent to me that much difficulty in trying to understand the Scriptures could be avoided if we would first of all recognize the

58

identity of the original recipients. As we understand to whom these words were written and study to understand as best we can their contemporary circumstances, then we can more properly consider how these writings impacted them. Rather than transferring the direction of the author's message to ourselves and our own times, we learn from the specific situation of the original readers in relation to the instruction and information contained in the message. Much of the writing that is included in the canon of Scripture is "occasional" in nature. In other words it was written for a specific occasion or to address a specific situation. If we do not grasp this, we will necessarily fail to grasp the true meaning and intent of the message of these documents, and potentially apply them in ways that may well be inappropriate. When we tear these writings from their original context, we will certainly distort their message.

To state that the preterist position is based only, or even primarily on the three texts that the writer noted above, is either dishonest or a gross display of ignorance. Although Matthew 24:34 and its parallels in Mark and Luke are extremely important passages with which every Bible student must grapple, they are by no means the only passages supporting fulfilled eschatology. Numerous other passages clearly express the anticipated imminence of Christ's coming and the end of the age. This imminence should be expected since all of the New Testament writings reflect and are guided by the teachings of Jesus. The New Testament writers use a wide variety of words and phrases to convey this sense of imminence and are not dependent upon the word *genea* to express this concept. The many different ways that imminence is presented in the NT epistles only serves to strengthen the position that *"this generation"* indeed speaks of those living at the time Jesus walked upon the earth; His contemporaries.

It has been my experience in recent years that many who attempt to critique and condemn the preterist model of eschatology have not taken sufficient time to familiarize themselves with and give serious consideration to the teachings and explanations of leading proponents of this perspective. Frequently the arguments made against fulfilled eschatology are thoroughly addressed in a wealth of preterist writings. My impression is that in many cases, those who critique have only a cursory understanding of what they are attacking. Most, if not all of the leading preterist teachers and writers have come out of other "systems," whether dispensationalism, amillennialism, postmillennialism, etc. For this reason, many of them have an in-depth knowledge of the systems out of which they have come. They are more readily able to critique the systems they left (which in many cases they had embraced and taught for many years), whereas those who critique preterism must invest considerable time and I think, more honestly engage those whose system they challenge so as to come to a more thorough and reasonable understanding of this system. It seems to me that this is their Christian duty and responsibility if they would attempt to provide truly fair and honest criticism, and ultimately expose it (as many claim) as heretical.

In a number of instances when books or articles have been written critical of fulfilled eschatology, the authors of these books have declined to interact with those they criticize. In many cases, those they have targeted have responded and sought without success, opportunities to fairly debate the important issues that have been brought into question in these books and articles. In a way this is not only unworthy of one professing to be a follower of Christ, it is also in a sense un-American (not legally, but in principle) by not allowing the accused to face his accuser.

Then They Shall Know That I Am The Lord

Having dealt with "preliminaries" related to the timing of Christ's second coming, let us move on to focus on the primary theme of this extended work. There are statements made by Jesus that seldom receive due attention and yet these statements tie in intimately with what is no doubt a major theme pertaining to the identity of God and ultimately the true identity of Christ Jesus.

Before moving forward, please consider the opening words of the passage just discussed. After hearing the powerful words spoken by Jesus in Matthew 23, his disciples drew His attention to the temple. Jesus then spoke to them of its coming desolation. As they mulled over His words on their ascent of the Mount of Olives, they were prompted to ask a very important question: "Tell us, when will these things be? And what will be the sign of Your coming (presence, ST), and of the end the age?" (Matthew 24:3). Keep in your mind the following comment from Don Preston in response to this verse, as this study progresses toward its conclusion: "Note that the disciples asked for the "sign" of Jesus' parousia. They were asking to know what visible event would prove that he was present and active. The visible reality of the invasions in view were the "sign" that YHVH was at work."

It is not uncommon for proponents of Covenant Eschatology to be asked about the fulfillment of Philippians 2:9-11 where Paul said: "Therefore God also has highly exalted Him and given Him the name which is above every name, that at the name of Jesus every knee should bow, of those in heaven, and of those on earth, and of those under the earth, and that every tongue should confess that Jesus Christ is Lord, to the glory of God the Father" (Philippians 2:9-11).

61

The question may be asked: "If you truly believe that all prophecy has been fulfilled, how do you explain the fulfillment of Paul's words in this passage?" A careful reading of this passage however, might prompt another question: "Is this really a prophecy or is it a statement of what God has already done, and because of that what should be the response of all who hear His name?" Paul quoted from chapter 45 of the prophecy of Isaiah and there are other passages from that section of the prophecy that must also be considered in the overall context of that passage. This context as well as the entire stream of Paul's message in this section of his letter to the Philippians must be examined closely in order to see exactly what he does say and what he means by what he said.

Is this passage a prediction that at some point in Paul's future there would be a moment in time when there was to be a temporal event where everyone in totality (in heaven, earth, under the earth) would bow their knee and publicly confess that Jesus is Lord? This seems to be the implication behind the original question. Is it perhaps a more biblically faithful understanding (one that is consistent with a scriptural pattern established throughout the Old Testament scriptures) to say that Paul is declaring in much the same way as the Old Covenant prophets, that God *had* exalted Jesus and given Him the name which is above every name?

If that is the proper understanding, then based on what God had done, Jesus was due the same honor and glory that was owed the Father. That this exaltation had taken place would be demonstrated, confirmed or manifested as Jesus fulfilled the promise made numerous times during his earthly ministry to come in judgment against the unbelieving of Jerusalem.

Look here at two significant passages from Isaiah:

62

"I am the Lord, that is My name; and My glory I will not give to another, nor My praise to carved images" (Isaiah 42:8).

"For My own sake, for My own sake, I will do it; for how should My name be profaned? And I will not give My glory to another" (Isaiah 48:11).

These statements of God spoken through his prophet Isaiah are very significant to this discussion. The LORD is God's name, not a title. It uniquely identified God, and His name and glory was not to be shared with any other being. See the comments below from a sermon by David Curtis who is the Pastor of the Berean Bible Church of Virginia Beach, Virginia.

"Let me say a word about the name Jehovah. In Hebrew Scripture the personal name of God is written with four Hebrew letters -- yod, heh, vav, heh (YHWH)-- and therefore called the *tetragrammaton*. This name appears 6,829 times in the Hebrew Scriptures.

In the First Temple period, at least until the Babylonian Exile in 586 B.C., the divine name was regularly pronounced in daily life. By the third century B.C., although the *tetragrammaton* was pronounced by priests in certain Temple liturgies, Jews avoided its use, employing instead many other substitutes. When reading or reciting Scripture, the custom was to substitute *'adonai* (LORD).

Until the early Middle Ages, Hebrew was written without vowels. By the sixth century A.D. a system of vowel signs

63

was developed by the Masoretes, the Jewish scholars of the period, to aid the reader in pronunciation. They superimposed the vowel signs of the word *'adonai* upon the four consonants of God's name.

In 1518 A.D. in his, *A Monumental Work of Christian Mysticism*, the Italian theologian and Franciscan friar Galatinus, not realizing that the Masoretes had placed the vowel signs of another word with the consonants *yhwh*, fused the vowels of *adonai* with the consonants of the divine name and thus gave the Church "Jehovah," a word which has no meaning in Hebrew. So strike the word Jehovah from your Christian vocabulary, it is not biblical at all."

As is discussed shortly, Jesus told His disciples in Matthew 16:27 that He would come in the glory of the Father. Jesus however, was given that name and was to share God's glory when He came in judgment. So based on the passages from Isaiah cited above which say that God will not give His name or glory to another, there must be contradiction to these statements, or *there is in fact a unique oneness of equality between the LORD and His Son* (Servant).

Throughout the Gospel accounts are found instances where the Jewish leaders rejected and condemned Jesus because of statements He made which they perceived to be claims to be one with God. In response to these statements they plotted how they might kill him (Matthew 26:3-4; Luke 22:1-2; John 5:18; John 10:25-33). Therefore the dispute over Jesus' true identity was/is the major issue. It is what ultimately led to His crucifixion. As Jesus stood before Caiaphas and the council, they rejected His claims and determined that He was deserving of death (Matthew 26:65). This conclusion was in response

64

to Jesus' statement in Matthew 26:64, which to them was a clear claim of equality with God and a pronouncement that He would come in judgment against them. How Jesus would vindicate these remarkable claims is the matter which will be addressed in what follows. This issue should be of immense import to all.

Following are several passages from Isaiah's prophecy that speak to this specific discussion. The first is the passage that Paul quoted in Philippians and these verses describe how the LORD sends forth His word and that it does not return unfulfilled. Because that is true, every knee shall bow, every tongue shall take an oath, all because of the LORD's faithfulness in fulfilling His word. That to Paul is why all should bow their knee and confess that Jesus is LORD. God had exalted His Son and given Him a name (LORD) that was above every name. Jesus had sent forth His word and would shortly bring it to pass so that it would not return unfulfilled.

"Tell and bring forth your case; yes, let them take counsel together. Who has declared this from ancient time? Who has told it from that time? Have not I, the Lord? And there is no other God besides Me, a just God and a Savior; there is none besides Me. 'Look to Me, and be saved, all you ends of the earth! For I am God, and there is no other. I have sworn by Myself; the word has gone out of My mouth in righteousness, and shall not return, that to Me every knee shall bow, every tongue shall take an oath. He shall say, 'surely in the Lord I have righteousness and strength. To Him men shall come, and all shall be ashamed who are incensed against Him. In the Lord all the descendants of Israel shall be justified, and shall glory.'" (Isaiah 45:21-25)

Isaiah 52 ties directly to the amazing prophecy of chapter 53, and pointed to the time that Paul described when God's Servant would be "exalted and extolled and be very high." It then begins the wonderful description of the suffering servant that carries over into chapter 53 where the ministry of Christ is displayed in all of its glory as the prophet tells how God's Servant "was wounded for our transgressions, He was bruised for our iniquities; the chastisement for our peace was upon Him, and by His stripes we are healed" (Isaiah 53:5).

"Behold, My Servant shall deal prudently; He shall be exalted and extolled and be very high. Just as many were astonished at you, so His visage was marred more than any man, and His form more than the sons of men; so shall He sprinkle many nations. Kings shall shut their mouths at Him; for what had not been told them they shall see, and what they had not heard they shall consider" (Isaiah 52:13-15).

The next two texts are from earlier in Isaiah's prophecy and establish this important concept that God is exalted in judgment. The first from chapter 5 makes this point explicit, while the passage from chapter 2 is no less forceful, although not quite as direct. "That day" referred to multiple times in chapter 2 is clearly a day of judgment, and in that day the LORD will be exalted.

"People shall be brought down, each man shall be humbled, and the eyes of the lofty shall be humbled. But the Lord of hosts shall be exalted in judgment, and God who is holy shall be hallowed in righteousness" (Isaiah 5:15-16).

66

"The lofty looks of man shall be humbled, the haughtiness of men shall be bowed down, and the Lord alone shall be exalted in that day. For the day of the LORD of hosts shall come upon everything proud and lofty, upon everything lifted up-- and it shall be brought low... The loftiness of man shall be bowed down, and the haughtiness of men shall be brought low; the LORD alone will be exalted in that day" (Isaiah 2:11-12,17).

In Matthew 16:27, Jesus said: "For the Son of Man will come in the glory of His Father with His angels, and then He will reward each according to his works." The fact that He said that He would "reward each according to his works," indicated that this was to be a coming in judgment. Also inherent in this statement and consistent with the biblical pattern, was that God's glory is manifest in the judgment of His enemies. The Father had been the One who poured out judgment throughout the Old Testament, but we find described in the New Testament a fascinating "transfer of power."

"For as the Father raises the dead and gives life to them, even so the Son gives life to whom He will. For the Father judges no one, but has committed all judgment to the Son, that all should honor the Son just as they honor the Father. He who does not honor the Son does not honor the Father who sent Him" (John 5:21-23).

Jesus' words seem clear and what He said echoes a concept that is developed in the Old Testament writings. In order for the Son to be honored as the Father is honored, for His name to be above every name, it would be necessary that He too come in judgment. Throughout His earthly ministry, and in particular in the Olivet Discourse, Jesus pointed to just such a soon coming judgment. This

67

to Paul is why all "should confess that Jesus Christ is Lord, to the glory of the Father."

Despite the undoubted truth of this assertion, there is an interesting statement found later in John's Gospel that must cause us to reflect a bit. "And if anyone hears My words and does not believe, I do not judge him; for I did not come to judge the world but to save the world" (John 12:47). Jesus came into the earthly realm as a man. This is something that "orthodox" Christianity has affirmed throughout its history. His earthly ministry culminated in His being offered up as the perfect sacrifice for the sin of the world (John 1:29). He came to save, not to judge, but in order to vindicate His claims to be one with God all judgment had been committed to Him.

Throughout the Old Testament, prophets were sent to call the nation of Israel to repentance. This call to repentance along with the prophet's descriptions of the consequence of not heeding this call, were the overwhelming message that God spoke through His servants.

There is an interesting and very important distinction that can be made between the Old Testament prophets (including John the Baptist) and Jesus as a prophet. When the prophets preached judgment, they always pointed away from themselves and toward God as the source of judgment. Throughout the Gospels, Jesus is seen pointing to Himself as the one who would bring judgment. This is a clear self-identification with His Father in heaven, and when he made statements such as, "you will see the Son of Man sitting at the right hand of the Power, and coming on the clouds of heaven" (Matthew 26:64), the ones who heard Him understood it precisely in that way.

As one who may be seen as the last of the Old Covenant prophets, John the Baptist came preaching a message that fit well within the pattern established by the Old Testament prophets.

"And he went into all the region around the Jordan, preaching a baptism of repentance for the remission of sins, . . . Then he said to the multitudes that came out to be baptized by him, 'Brood of vipers! Who warned you to flee from the wrath to come? Bear fruits in keeping with repentance. And do not begin to say to yourselves, 'We have Abraham as our father.' For I tell you, God is able from these stones to raise up children for Abraham. Even now the axe is laid to the root of the trees. Every tree therefore that does not bear good fruit is cut down and thrown into the fire" (Luke 3:3, 7-9).

Again, John used the Greek word *mello* in the phrase translated here as the "wrath to come," and as has been noted previously this word actually denotes imminence and means "about to come," or as Strong's defines it: "to be on the point of doing or suffering something." It is worth re-emphasizing that this word is used numerous times in the New Testament, but in many critical passages many modern translations do not fully bring out this aspect of the word's predominant meaning. Notice also that he made the following statement within the same immediate context: "Even now the axe is laid to the root of the trees." This image clearly emphasizes and reinforces the urgency and sense of immediacy of the situation.

Jesus began His earthly ministry in much the same way as John. "From that time Jesus began to preach and to say, 'Repent, for the kingdom of heaven is at hand'" (Matthew 4:17). Later as He neared the time of His crucifixion (Matthew 12:34; 23:33), Jesus used the

69

same "brood of vipers" imagery as had John the Baptist in condemning His own generation, and as He warned them of impending judgment.

"Therefore you are witnesses against yourselves that you are sons of those who murdered the prophets. Fill up, then, the measure of your fathers' guilt. Serpents, brood of vipers! How can you escape the condemnation of hell? Therefore, indeed, I send you prophets, wise men, and scribes: some of them you will kill and crucify, and some of them you will scourge in your synagogues and persecute from city to city, that on you may come all the righteous blood shed on the earth, from the blood of righteous Abel to the blood of Zechariah, son of Berechiah, whom you murdered between the temple and the altar. Assuredly, I say to you, all these things will come upon this generation" (Matthew 23:31- 36).

This message continued through the ministry of His disciples as is testified in the book of Acts and throughout the New Testament epistles. This is seen in the Apocalypse as well. Indeed Peter's sermon on the day of Pentecost pointed specifically to this. His ministry began with the same message that John the Baptist and his Lord had preached. "And Peter said to them, 'Repent and be baptized every one of you in the name of Jesus Christ for the forgiveness of your sins'... And with many other words he testified and exhorted them, saying, 'Be saved from this perverse generation.'" (Acts 2:38, 40). Note that Peter made reference to the same "perverse" generation that He had heard his Lord mention multiple times.

Jesus called His contemporary generation to repent. Many, especially the Jewish leaders (although Acts 6:7 reports that many of the Priests were obedient to the faith), did not heed His call. Indeed they filled up the measure of their fathers' guilt by killing Jesus, and later by persecuting and killing the "prophets, wise men, and scribes" that He sent to them. Because of their obstinate refusal to listen to His words, they came under condemnation. Moses had warned Israel centuries before of a prophet to come; a prophet they would reject at their own risk.

"And the LORD said to me: 'What they have spoken is good. I will raise up for them a Prophet like you from among their brethren, and will put My words in His mouth, and He shall speak to them all that I command Him. And it shall be that whoever will not hear My words, which He speaks in My name, I will require it of him'" (Deuteronomy 18:17-19).

That Moses was in fact pointing to Jesus was confirmed by Peter in Acts 3:18-23.

"But those things which God foretold by the mouth of all His prophets, that the Christ would suffer, He has thus fulfilled. Repent therefore and be converted, that your sins may be blotted out, so that times of refreshing may come from the presence of the Lord, and that He may send Jesus Christ, who was preached to you before, whom heaven must receive until the times of restoration of all things, which God has spoken by the mouth of all His holy prophets since the world began. For Moses truly said to the fathers, 'The LORD your God will raise up for you a Prophet like me from your brethren. Him you shall hear in all things, whatever He says to you. And it shall be that every soul who will not hear that Prophet shall be utterly destroyed from among the people.'"

Notice that Peter said that all those who would not hear that Prophet (who was Jesus) would be destroyed from among the people. The phrase "the people" is frequently used in the scriptures to designate Israel. They considered themselves to be THE PEOPLE because of their privileged position before God, and Paul confirmed this when he spoke in Romans 9:4 of his countrymen according to the flesh, "who are Israelites, to whom pertain the adoption, the glory, the covenants, the giving of the law, the service of God, and the promises." Peter told those men of Israel (Acts 3:12) that whoever would not hear (or believe in) Jesus would be cut off from the true people of God. In other words, belief in Jesus as the Messiah was the identifying mark of the true people of God. It was not according to physical birth, but rather spiritual birth.

Many who heard Peter's message that day did turn to God through Jesus Christ. Sadly many others of that generation did not, and as they continued in the hardness of their hearts they sealed their own fate. There is a passage in Hosea that seems to me to tie directly to what was taking place as people turned to Israel's Christ in these 1st century times. Hosea's prophecy and the promises found therein were directed to Israel. In chapter 5, God pointed to a coming judgment of Israel and said,

> "For I will be like a lion to Ephraim, and like a young lion to the house of Judah. I, even I, will tear them and go away; I will take them away, and no one shall rescue. I will return again to My place till they acknowledge their offense. Then they will seek My face" (Hosea 5:14-15).

72

God said He would tear Israel and take them away, and then He would go away to His place. He would leave them and would not return to them until they acknowledged their offense, and at that time they (Israel) would seek His face. This prophecy was being fulfilled in the 1st century through the ministry of Jesus and His disciples as they preached this message of repentance. They were calling Israel to acknowledge their offense against their God and to seek His face. The testimony of the early chapters of Acts confirms that it was "men of Israel" who did in fact repent and turn to the Lord. In its very earliest days, the church (those who repented and turned to the Lord) consisted exclusively of Jews who resided in Jerusalem, or who had come to Jerusalem to celebrate the feast of Pentecost.

Jesus promised that He would come "in the glory of His Father." He told Caiaphas and the Sanhedrin that they would "see the Son of Man sitting at the right hand of the Power, and coming on the clouds of heaven." The straightforward reading of Jesus' words indicated that all this was to take place before all of His disciples, Caiaphas, and the members of the Sanhedrin would die. As we saw earlier Jesus told the Jews:

> "The Son can do nothing of Himself, but what He sees the Father do; for whatever He does, the Son also does in like manner. For the Father loves the Son, and shows Him all things that He Himself does; and He will show Him greater works than these, that you may marvel. For as the Father raises the dead and gives life to them, even so the Son gives life to whom He will. For the Father judges no one, but has committed all judgment to the Son, that all should honor the Son just as they honor the Father. He who does not honor the Son does not honor the Father who sent Him" (John 5:19-23).

73

The eternal Son of God (John 1:1-2) had seen the Father come in judgment many times before, and now He would do the same "in like manner." By coming in judgment against Jerusalem in AD70, Jesus vindicated the innocent blood of all the martyrs down through the ages (Matthew 23:29-36). He also vindicated His claim to be the Son of God who had assumed the prerogative of judgment so that He too should receive the same honor and glory as His Father.

Not only did Jesus judge that wicked generation, he also delivered the true children of God from the persecution that they had been experiencing from that very same generation of Jews. He gave them signs so that as they faithfully watched (as Jesus had repeatedly told them to do) they would know when the time was at hand and could therefore escape the coming wrath.

Just as the Father had repeatedly revealed Himself as the Lord when he came in deliverance and judgment, Jesus claimed that He would do the same. The early church had been severely persecuted and the initial persecution was from the unbelieving Jews, including the likes of Saul of Tarsus (Acts 4:18; 5:28; 7:52-60; 8:1; 9:1-2; 17:5; 24; 1 Thessalonians 2:14). This pattern continued up until Jerusalem was destroyed. Many historians agree that even Nero's persecution of Christians was instigated to a great extent by Jews who rejected Jesus as Messiah.

The destruction of Jerusalem and the dispersion of the Jews who were not killed during the war, ended a major source of persecution for the church. It also revealed to those who would see, the Christians as the true sons of God. In Galatians chapter 4, Paul used the story of Isaac and Ishmael as an allegory, distinguishing between the children of the flesh and the children of promise (those who were born according to

74

the Spirit). He noted that even as Ishmael had persecuted Isaac, now fleshly Israel was persecuting "Spiritual Israel." "But, as he who was born according to the flesh then persecuted him who was born according to the Spirit, even so it is now" (Galatians 4:29). Paul clearly saw what took place with Isaac and Ishmael as analogous to what was taking place in his day.

The contrast was now between those of Old Covenant Israel who had rejected their Messiah, and those who were in Christ through faith. He went on in the next verse to state, "Nevertheless what does the Scripture say? 'Cast out the bondwoman and her son, for the son of the bondwoman shall not be heir with the son of the freewoman'" (Galatians 4:30). In verse 25, Paul said that in this allegory the bondwoman and her son, "corresponds to Jerusalem which now (1st century) *is.*" They were to be cast out. When this took place in A.D.70, fleshly Israel would no longer be able to persecute God's spiritual children. At the same time, it would be revealed that those who heeded the words of Jesus were the true "sons of God" (Romans 8:14-19, see also Hosea 1:10-11).

According to the writings of Paul, the Christians in Thessalonica were suffering great persecution. In 2 Thessalonians 1:4-8 He wrote:

> "That we ourselves boast of you among the churches of God for your patience and faith in all your persecutions and tribulations that you endure, which is manifest evidence of the righteous judgment of God, that you may be counted worthy of the kingdom of God, for which you also suffer; since it is a righteous thing with God to repay with tribulation those who trouble you, and to give you who are troubled rest with us when the Lord Jesus is revealed from

heaven with His mighty angels, in flaming fire taking vengeance on those who do not know God, and on those who do not obey the gospel of our Lord Jesus Christ."

Paul told those saints that God would repay those who troubled *them* (not some group of people thousands of years later), and He would give *them* (the Thessalonian saints) rest when the Lord Jesus was revealed from heaven. This promise was made to those 1st century Thessalonians who were experiencing persecution. Is it faithful to the text to interpret it any other way? The expectation was that they would witness the coming (presence) of the Lord Jesus, who by coming in judgment would be revealed as the Son of God, the King of kings and Lord of lords (Revelation 17:14, 19:16). He would then deliver *them* from their suffering and take vengeance on those who did not know God.

When God delivered His people from their bondage of slavery in Egypt, He said "the Egyptians shall know that I am the LORD, when I stretch out My hand on Egypt and bring out the children of Israel from among them" (Exodus 7:5). Hundreds of years later, Ezekiel was told by God to warn Judah of their impending judgment. "Then the cities that are inhabited shall be laid waste, and the land shall become desolate; and you shall know that I am the LORD" (Ezekiel 12:20). In contrast God told the faithful remnant: "You shall know that I am the LORD, when I bring you into the land of Israel, into the country for which I raised My hand in an oath to give to your fathers" (Ezekiel 20:42).

God's glory was manifested throughout the Old Testament through His judgments, as well as in the deliverance of the vessels of His mercy. As was seen earlier, Isaiah 5:16 stated: "The Lord of hosts shall be exalted in judgment." In the same manner, Jesus would

76

reveal Himself as the Son of God and would be exalted as the King of Kings and the Lord of Lords. Psalm 9:16 says: "The LORD is known by the judgment He executes." He would manifest His glory through the promised judgment of His enemies, and in the deliverance of those who "heard" His message of repentance. The temple and old Jerusalem with it, as symbols of the Old Covenant, would be destroyed and the Old Covenant would fully pass away.

It is not uncommon to find passages in the Old Testament with descriptive phrases that speak about God as if He was coming "out of His place," or coming "from afar." In Isaiah 64:1-3, the prophet called upon God to come down as He had done before.

"Oh, that You would rend the heavens! That You would come down! That the mountains might shake at Your presence-- As fire burns brushwood, as fire causes water to boil-- *To make Your name known to Your adversaries*, that the nations may tremble at *Your presence!* When You did awesome things for which we did not look, You came down, the mountains shook at Your presence." (My emphasis)

Here is a reference to God coming down and making His presence known to the nations. Yet He was never optically or visibly seen by any human eye. His presence was manifested in the judgment of His enemies, and according to this text, this is how He would make His name known. Likewise Jesus' presence (Greek word *Parousia:* I. presence; II. the coming, arrival, advent) and coming was to be manifested in the judgment of His enemies (unbelieving Jews), as well as in the vindication of the martyrs through the destruction of Judah and Jerusalem by the Roman armies.

77

Note that in Isaiah, God's presence is not a visible presence but rather God's presence *manifested through judgment*. The prophet was speaking of things that God had done in the past. While there are passages that speak metaphorically of God going up out of Seir and marching from the region of Edom (Judges 5:3), or say that He bowed the heavens and come down with thick darkness under His feet (2 Samuel 21:10), few if any commentators understand these passages as describing the "literal" physical presence of God.

Considering this OT background, the modern reader should understand that many of the statements made by our Lord use the same sense of language as we find in the Old Testament. It is almost impossible to believe that those who heard Jesus say these things in the first century would not have associated these statements with similar words that had been spoken by their prophets. It is highly unlikely that they would have expected a "literal" fulfillment, as is so commonly the case today, of these apocalyptic images used by Jesus in the New Testament.

Acceptance of the figurative nature of the language used to describe Jesus' coming (or presence), should help ease the internal tension in the minds of many modern Christians who can easily see that there are a multitude of indications within the New Testament of the expectation of a climactic event in the first century timeframe. It will help the modern reader more fully appreciate and embrace the pervasive sense of the 1st century imminence of these events that are clearly found in numerous passages throughout this text. The diligence and the consistent sense of urgency with which Jesus and His disciples proclaimed this soon coming judgment and deliverance can not only be gladly acknowledged, but the recognition of His faithful 1st century fulfillment can now bring about a glorious celebration within the believer's heart.

Church history shows that all the signs that Jesus gave to His disciples have been proclaimed to be coming to pass in generation after generation over the course of history. This despite the fact that Jesus said that "all these things" would happen during and specifically to the generation to whom He spoke. A close study of the writings of Flavius Josephus demonstrates the remarkable fulfillment, in the years leading up to A.D.70, of these signs that Jesus had given His disciples. There is also significant scriptural support for this as well. (John Bray's book *Matthew 24 Fulfilled* is an excellent resource documenting from many sources the fulfillment of Matthew 24 in the 1st century.)

When surveying the signs given in the early verses of Matthew 24, it should be noted that there are also listed several events and natural disasters that were likely not intended to be understood as apocalyptic in nature. Indeed, if the context in which these signs were given is ignored, it would be understandable that generation after generation would have "seen" these signs being fulfilled in their day.

"And you will hear of wars and rumors of wars. See that you are not troubled; for all these things must come to pass, but the end is not yet. For nation will rise against nation, and kingdom against kingdom. And there will be famines, pestilences, and earthquakes in various places. All these are the beginning of sorrows. "Then they will deliver you up to tribulation and kill you, and you will be hated by all nations for My name's sake" (Matthew 24:6-9).

There is nothing unique about wars and rumors of war; nothing unusual about nation rising against nation and kingdom against kingdom; certainly in that day nothing unusual about famines, pestilence, and earthquakes. All of those things have been more or less ubiquitous events at various times and in various places throughout the last two millennia. Had Jesus not given His disciples a definite timeframe for the occurrence of "these things," it could be supposed that it would be quite reasonable for any number of generations to have believed that they were living in the "last days." The truth is however, that it does not matter whether any of these signs were seen in any generation following after the generation in which Jesus lived. Jesus clearly placed a limitation on the timeframe in which the signs would be observed. He said in words that could hardly be any more straightforward and clear, that "this generation will by no means pass away till all these things take place" (Matthew 24:34). Once that generation passed, those signs were no longer of any relevance to biblical eschatology.

With these warnings, it is most likely that Jesus was actually intending to prevent the type of response observed so frequently in subsequent generations, in which it seems that almost every natural disaster, every political or civil upheaval has led to renewed cries that the end is near.

Sadly this tendency has returned with a vengeance, and yet again in our day many prophecy "experts" are convinced that this (our 21st century generation) is the terminal generation, the generation that shall see "all these things" come to pass. How we miss the gracious nature of Jesus' warnings when we fail to apprehend that he was preparing His contemporaries so that they would escape the great tribulation that was about to come upon Judah and Jerusalem. He was giving His "friends" (John 15:15) special instructions so that they would not be caught unawares when He came in judgment upon that 1st century generation. As the Great Shepherd, He was preparing these 1st century disciples, His precious "little flock" (Luke 12:32), for a future to be filled with many difficulties, but He also encouraged them with the assurance that *they* would find relief. He repeatedly assured them that if they were watchful, they would be saved. When they saw Jerusalem surrounded they were to flee and not enter into the city.

He was not looking into the indefinite future to some unknown group who would someday experience the "Great Tribulation." He was preparing His disciples so that when they saw the things He described, they could "flee to the mountains" and escape the "days of vengeance." He was addressing a generation spoken of specifically by the Old Testament prophets (see 1 Peter 1:12 and Acts 3:24).

"But when *you* see Jerusalem surrounded by armies, then know that its desolation is near. Then let those who are in Judea flee to the mountains, let those who are in the midst of her depart, and let not those who are in the country enter her. For these are the days of vengeance, that all things which are written may be fulfilled" (Luke 21:20-22).

It is critical to understand that He was speaking to a specific group of people. He said: "when *you* see" these things. He did not say "if," but "when." It was certain that they (this 1st generation) would see Jerusalem surrounded by armies. He wasn't talking about an unspecified people. He was speaking to His disciples with the intent that they would take heed of His words and that they would then share this message with their contemporaries. Just as Noah had a message to preach, Jesus' disciples were called to share His message. That 1st century generation was the anti-type of Noah's generation. This message is exactly what we find in the preaching recorded in the

81

book of Acts, as well as the message found within many of the letters of the New Testament.

If language had any definite meaning to those to whom Jesus' words were originally spoken - and how could it not? - then it is beyond dispute that Jesus' warning was to those who were hearing His voice in the first century. When they (1st century disciples) saw Jerusalem surrounded by armies, they were to know that its desolation was near. They would also know that the time in which they were living was the "days of vengeance, that all things which are written may be fulfilled." These were clearly things that were to happen in that 1st century generation, and yet many commentators wish to push these things out thousands of years because what happened in AD70 does not precisely conform to their preconceived ideas of how Jesus' words should be fulfilled.

When Jesus made His statement regarding the "days of vengeance" and then said that when those days came all things which were written would be fulfilled, there must be a context to which He spoke. Considering the identity of His audience in this specific section of Luke's gospel, and understanding the link to Matthew 23 and Jesus' vehement condemnation of Jerusalem's religious leaders, it all but demands that He was speaking of and predicting the imminent fulfillment of covenant judgment that had been written of in the Old Covenant scriptures. It must surely be associated with the *"vengeance of the covenant"* spoken of in Leviticus 26:25 (refer to the Appendix for a more in depth discussion of this passage).

"Then, if you walk contrary to Me, and are not willing to obey Me, I will bring on you seven times more plagues, according to your sins. I will also send wild beasts among you, which

82

shall rob you of your children, destroy your livestock, and make you few in number; and your highways shall be desolate. And if by these things you are not reformed by Me, but walk contrary to Me, then I also will walk contrary to you, and I will punish you yet seven times for your sins. And I will bring a sword against you that will execute the vengeance of the covenant; when you are gathered together within your cities I will send pestilence among you; and you shall be delivered into the hand of the enemy" (Leviticus 26:21-25).

Numerous passages in the New Testament point to the fact that Jesus saw Himself as a prophet and more specifically as the penultimate prophet like unto Moses that God said He would send to His people (Deuteronomy 18:15). He was the prophet of whom Peter said; "every soul who will not hear that Prophet shall be utterly destroyed from among the people" (Acts 3:23). From this it would appear that Jesus was a prophet whose message was certainly one warning of judgment just like His predecessors. It would not be surprising if the tenor of His message was similar as well.

Moses' words to Israel as they prepared to enter and possess the land of Canaan is prophetic of Israel's future, and has as its basis the law of blessing and cursing found in Leviticus 26 and Deuteronomy 28. These passages are the foundation for the message of much of the forthcoming Old Testament prophecies as well as those found in the New Testament.

"For they are a nation void of counsel, nor is there any understanding in them. Oh, that they were wise, that they understood this, that they would consider their latter end! How could one chase a thousand, and two put ten thousand to

83

flight, unless their Rock had sold them, and the Lord had surrendered them? For their rock is not like our Rock, even our enemies themselves being judges. For their vine is of the vine of Sodom and of the fields of Gomorrah; their grapes are grapes of gall, their clusters are bitter. Their wine is the poison of serpents, and the cruel venom of cobras. Is this not laid up in store with Me, sealed up among My treasures? Vengeance is Mine, and recompense; their foot shall slip in due time; for the day of their calamity is at hand, and the things to come hasten upon them. For the Lord will judge His people and have compassion on His servants, when He sees that their power is gone, and there is no one remaining, bond or free. He will say: 'Where are their gods, the rock in which they sought refuge? Who ate the fat of their sacrifices, and drank the wine of their drink offering? Let them rise and help you, and be your refuge. Now see that I, even I, am He, and there is no God besides Me; I kill and I make alive; I wound and I heal; nor is there any who can deliver from My hand. For I raise My hand to heaven, And say, 'As I live forever, If I whet My glittering sword, and My hand takes hold on judgment, I will render vengeance to My enemies, and repay those who hate Me. I will make My arrows drunk with blood, and My sword shall devour flesh, with the blood of the slain and the captives, from the heads of the leaders of the enemy.'" "Rejoice, O Gentiles, with His people; for He will avenge the blood of His servants, and render vengeance to His adversaries; He will provide atonement for His land and His people." (Deuteronomy 32:28-43).

This prophecy was directed to Israel in the context of looking forward to her last days. 1st century Israel's response to Jesus clearly revealed

84

them to be God's adversaries, described by Moses, who would soon experience the covenant vengeance of God.

As previously noted, John MacArthur has at times been a notable critic of covenant, or fulfilled eschatology (preterism), and has authored a book offered as a critique of the preterist position. He has readily acknowledged in his writings that Jerusalem was surrounded by armies in AD70 and that Jerusalem was sacked by Rome in that famous and devastating siege. He even quotes from Josephus' description of those horrible days. However, because of his view of how Jesus' prophecy must be fulfilled, he is forced to deny Jesus' words regarding the timing of these events. He says, "Yet those were not, in the words of Luke 21:22, 'the days of vengeance, (when) all things which are written may be fulfilled.' Christ did not return visibly in AD70. The opposing armies were not defeated by His presence. All Israel was not saved. The Jews were not grafted back into the olive tree. There is much pertaining to the Day of the Lord and His vengeance against sin that yet awaits fulfillment" (MacArthur, *The Second Coming*, p.104). Rather than acknowledge Jesus' use of language, images and concepts found in numerous prophetic passages in the Old Testament and then re-examine the nature of his expectations, MacArthur is forced to deny the obvious meaning of the words of Jesus. He goes on to state that Jerusalem had been surrounded by armies many times in subsequent years. He even goes so far as to say that Jerusalem is "surrounded by armies" in a figurative sense in this present modern day (p.105).

It is critical that these things be put in their proper context. Jesus said to His disciples: "But when *you* see Jerusalem surrounded by armies, then know that its desolation is near." There is absolutely no doubt whatsoever that the Roman armies surrounded Jerusalem within that generation, and that Jerusalem was made completely desolate within that generation. In light of these historically verifiable facts, let us remember that Jesus had said that the days in which His disciples (1st century) saw Jerusalem surrounded by armies were to be *"the days of vengeance, that all things which are written may be fulfilled."* MacArthur counters that "there is much pertaining to the Day of the Lord and His vengeance against sin that yet awaits fulfillment." It would appear that MacArthur has developed his concept of vengeance apart from the context expressed and explained within the Scriptures. The Old Testament passages already cited are only two of a number of passages that address God's promise of vengeance against His enemies. MacArthur's own denial that Jesus fully poured out His vengeance as promised, unfortunately denies him of potentially his greatest apologetic tool in his debates with opponents of Christianity whether Jew, Moslem or atheist.

What is found written in the Old Covenant scriptures is the promise of vengeance against God's enemies from a covenantal context. The message of Deuteronomy 32 is the promise of vengeance to come against His enemies who in the context of the overall passage is unfaithful Israel who would be judged in their last days (Deuteronomy 31:29; 32:7, 20, 29).

Matthew 23 provides a detailed statement that must guide any understanding of the teaching that follows in Matthew 24ff. In it are spelled out the context and the target of the vengeance that was soon to be poured out. MacArthur does not seem to give Matthew 23 its due when developing his personal understanding and doctrine regarding God's vengeance. Diminishing the importance of Matthew 23 and not realizing its central importance to the immediate context of that section of Matthew's gospel can and will have a drastically negative impact on a proper understanding of not only the crucial passages that follow in Matthew 24-25, but on many other important

86

New Testament texts as well. As Jesus wrapped up his scathing rebuke of the Jews, He concluded with the following statement that should be our primary guide to developing a *biblically* accurate understanding of the topic of God's vengeance.

"Therefore, indeed, I send you prophets, wise men, and scribes: some of them you will kill and crucify, and some of them you will scourge in your synagogues and persecute from city to city, that on you may come all the righteous blood shed on the earth, from the blood of righteous Abel to the blood of Zechariah, son of Berechiah, whom you murdered between the temple and the altar. Assuredly, I say to you, all these things will come upon this generation" (Matthew 23:34-36).

In verse 38, Jesus then said: "See! Your house is left to you desolate." Understanding that the chapter break between chapters 23 and 24 is artificial, and not in the original text, means that this break does not require or even suggest a change in subject. Jesus continued to elaborate on this statement in the opening verses of chapter 24. The concluding words of chapter 23 are what precipitated the question asked by His disciples in Matthew 24:3, to which the remainder of Matthew 24 and 25 is His response.

"Then Jesus went out and departed from the temple, and His disciples came up to show Him the buildings of the temple. And Jesus said to them, 'Do you not see all these things? Assuredly, I say to you, not one stone shall be left here upon another, that shall not be thrown down'" (Matthew 24:1-2).

All of Jesus' teaching that followed in chapters 24 and 25, as well as that found in Mark 13 and Luke 21 must be understood as they related to His words in Matthew 23. Unfortunately, MacArthur does not seem to fully take into account this crucial section when developing his understanding of "the days of vengeance" (reference the Appendix). Failure to do so perverts his teaching on this issue. It causes him to essentially disregard and reject the incredibly important fulfillment of Jesus' promises that occurred in the events surrounding the destruction of Jerusalem in 70AD. Rather than understanding the limited context in which these words were given, MacArthur's presuppositions compel him to apply them on a global scale. Jesus' anguished cry in 23:37 would seem to place everything in its proper context: "O Jerusalem, Jerusalem, the one who kills the prophets and stones those who are sent to her!"

The fallacy of MacArthur's argument, as it is with all other futuristic speculation regarding the signs that Jesus gave to His disciples, is that it removes these teachings from the very specific context in which they were given and the particular situation that they were addressing. In light of Jesus' original words, it makes no difference what has taken place in subsequent generations that followed in the wake of that crucial 1st century generation. He spoke directly to His 1st century disciples and said, "So *you* also, when *you* see these things happening, know that the kingdom of God is near. Assuredly, I say to *you*, this generation will by no means pass away till all things take place" (Luke 21:32). Again, who was He telling to "know that the kingdom of God is near"? The generation of Jews alive in His day were the ones to whom His teachings were directed. They were the ones who were to see these things. If there were wars and rumors of wars, earthquakes, or armies surrounding Jerusalem in the 2nd, 3rd, 4th, etc. centuries, it really makes no difference as it relates to Jesus' prophesies.

It is well understood that throughout His earthly ministry, Jesus was confronted with unbelief. Many of the Jews who heard His message did not believe His claims to be the Son of God. Jesus certainly must have recognized that words come easy, and no doubt He understood the common modern truism that "actions speak louder than words." As He traveled about the region preaching the good news of God's faithfulness to Israel, He was performing signs and wonders, realizing that they would be a much more powerful testimony than just words alone. Much of what He did teach however, pointed to a time when He would come in judgment of that generation of Israel.

There is an important point to be made here about Jesus and miracles. It is often believed that his miracles proved that he is the Son of God. I believe this is misguided. While all of the signs and wonders he performed could be placed in the category of "works of My Father," there is no Biblical record of the Father actually walking about in bodily form performing miracles. This is important in light of the fact that Jesus said he was coming in the glory of the Father. He would come in judgment *as he had seen the Father judge*. And it was that judgment coming which would cause all men to honor him as they do the Father.

It is well established that other prophets such as Moses and Elijah performed miracles through the power of Yahweh, just as Jesus did during His earthly ministry. But their working of miracles did not identify them as "the Son of God." To be sure, their performance of miracles proved that they were sent by God, but to reiterate, their working of miracles did not identify them as *God*. For this reason we can say that the miracles Jesus performed did not confirm His divinity and status as the unique Son of God. They did serve to confirm His identity as a prophet, and perhaps even as Israel's Messiah (cf. John 7:31), and were presented as proof of that claim

(Matthew 11:2-6). However, Israel did not understand that Messiah was to be *God*!

The one great distinguishing work that Jesus would perform that would proclaim His divinity and status as the Son of God and as the LORD, would be His coming in judgment in the same manner as His Father had often done in the past. In John 10:37-38 Jesus said, "If I do not do the works of My Father, do not believe Me; but if I do, though you do not believe Me, believe the works, that you may know and believe that the Father is in Me, and I in Him." Although they did not believe His words, they did indeed fully understand the implications of His claim to be Son of God.

(We need to state clearly that Jesus also pointed to his coming resurrection as one of the key signs of his identity. Likewise, Paul affirmed that it was through Jesus' resurrection that he was "declared to be the Son of God, with power" (Romans 1:4). So Jesus actually gave two key signs of his deity - his resurrection and his parousia).

The biblical testimony indicates that Jesus' repeated claims, both explicit and implicit, to be the Son of God were the primary reason that the Jews sought to and eventually did kill Him (this statement should not be taken as anti-Semitic, but rather as a reflections of clear statements found in the New Testament passages such as Acts 2:22-23, 36, Acts 3:14-15, Acts 4:8-10, Acts 10:39, and 1 Thessalonians 2:14-15). "Therefore the Jews sought all the more to kill Him, because He not only broke the Sabbath, but also said that God was His Father, making Himself equal with God" (John 5:18).

In answer to Pilate's claim that he had found no fault in Jesus, the Jews answered him saying, "We have a law, and according to our law He ought to die, because He made Himself the Son of God"(John

19:7). ("And whoever blasphemes the name of the LORD shall surely be put to death. All the congregation shall certainly stone him, the stranger as well as him who is born in the land. When he blasphemes the name of the LORD, he shall be put to death." Leviticus 24:16) This was precisely the issue that caused the outcry from Caiaphas in Matthew 26:63-66.

Note also that in John 10:30 when Jesus said, "I and the Father are one," the Jews then took up stones to stone Him. In response to Jesus' query in verse 32 they said: "For a good work we do not stone You, but for blasphemy, and because You, being a Man, make Yourself God" (John 10:33). Although some today still deny this essential oneness with God, it was clear that the Jews of His day were quite certain that Jesus claimed to be equal with God, and was in fact claiming in some sense to be God. It is of great importance to note that when the Jews accused Him of making Himself God, Jesus never sought to correct them, if they were indeed in error in their understanding of the meaning of His words. It is reasonable to believe that the Jews understood very well what Jesus' words implied and that this was in fact His intent.

In order to vindicate His claims, Jesus had come with the purpose of doing the works of His Father. According to Jesus, it was His Father's desire that the Son should receive the same honor as the Father (John 5:23). As noted earlier, Paul told the Philippians:

"God also has highly exalted Him and given Him the name which is above every name, that at the name of Jesus every knee should bow, of those in heaven, and of those on earth, and of those under the earth, and that every tongue should confess that Jesus Christ is Lord, to the glory of God the Father" (Philippians 2:9-11).

The verses (vv. 5-8) prior to those cited above described how Jesus had been in the form of God, but had made Himself of no reputation, coming in the likeness of man. The incarnation had clearly and dramatically manifested Jesus as a man. But there was a need for something very different to demonstrate His equality with God. John 5:21-23 provided the template for accomplishing this before the "eyes" of His unbelieving generation as well as for a testimony to future generations.

From the verses cited above in Philippians chapter 2, it is quite evident that Paul believed that prior to His incarnation Jesus had existed in the form of God, but in coming to earth had "made Himself of no reputation, taking on the form of a bondservant, and coming in the likeness of men" (Philippians 2:6-7). As John 5:21-23 clearly indicates, Jesus claimed that His future (soon) coming in judgment would bring Him the same honor as the Father had received in His previous judgment comings. For those who insist that Jesus must come again in the form of a man, the question must be asked: "What is it about Jesus as a man coming in judgment that would differentiate Him from others such as Nebuchadnezzar or Sennacherib (or Titus for that matter) in whose 'hands' God had placed His sword of judgment?"

The writer of Hebrews explained the need for Jesus being "made a little lower than the angels" (Hebrews 2:5,7,9). It was specifically "for the suffering of death crowned with glory and honor, that He, by the grace of God, might taste death for everyone" (Hebrews 2:9). All Christians acknowledge that Jesus accomplished this on His

92

glorious cross, and according to the writer of Hebrews, it was the primary reason for His incarnation.

When Philip encountered the Ethiopian eunuch, he found him reading from Isaiah 53, which described the mission of God's Servant:

> "He was led as a sheep to the slaughter;
> And as a lamb before its shearer *is* silent,
> So He opened not His mouth.
> [33] In His humiliation His justice was taken away,
> And who will declare His generation?
> For His life is taken from the earth."
>
> (Acts 8:32-33)

God's purpose for the redemption of His people could only be fulfilled in this specific way as the Blessed Lamb of God, who became man, had His life taken from the earth. But once His redemptive work was accomplished, it was necessary to demonstrate that Jesus was one with the Father in all power and glory. The beautiful image of Jesus as the Lamb of God encompasses all the dimensions of His person. For the lamb to be slain, He must become man. "Inasmuch then as the children have partaken of flesh and blood, He Himself likewise shared in the same, that through death He might destroy him who had the power of death" (Hebrews 2:14).

But in Revelation chapters 21 and 22, the deity, the oneness of God and the Lamb, is displayed repeatedly (Revelation 21:14, 22-23 & Revelation 22:1, 3). The humanity and deity of Christ must be tied together, and His coming a second time as a man would in no way accomplish this task.

93

There is no doubt of the critical importance of Jesus' incarnation. Denial by some that Jesus had come in the flesh, was enough of a concern in those early days that it was mentioned in two of John's letters (1 John 4:2, 2 John 7), but certainly most of the Jews of His day knew Him as a man. But to them, that is all He was. That however, was not the question that would have been foremost in their minds. His repeated claim to be one with the Father was what needed to be supported, manifested, demonstrated and proved. Coming again as a man would have no impact on this issue and would not answer to the question of His deity – was He in fact King of kings, and Lord of lords? It was necessary for Him to follow the pattern set by the Father in order to convincingly reveal His true nature, identity and oneness with God.

No matter exactly how one interprets the apocalyptic visions of Jesus' second coming found in the New Testament, if a literalistic view is taken with Jesus as a man visibly riding on a horse or a cloud with a sword coming forth from His mouth, this is foreign to the pattern presented in the Hebrew scriptures of how God the Father "came" in judgment.

The material below demonstrates how, in Old Testament times, God had used men as the instrument of His judgment, but the fact that He accomplished His purposes through them, in no way demonstrated or even insinuated that they were in anyway equal with God. We can also say with certainty that these men were not deserving of the same honor as God. Likewise, Jesus coming in judgment as a man would do nothing to demonstrate His divine nature, or demand "that all should honor the Son just as they honor the Father" (John 5:23).

It may be helpful to review a representative passage from the Old Covenant scriptures that demonstrates very clearly the way that God

94

chose to reveal Himself, first through a prophetic message warning of judgment and then by the realization of that judgment through a chosen servant such as king Sennacherib of Assyria or king Nebuchadnezzar of Babylon. There are a number of places we could turn, but there is one remarkable passage early in Ezekiel's prophecy that I believe is uniquely appropriate.

Beginning in chapter 5, the prophet recorded that God spoke to him of the judgment that would soon come upon Judah and Jerusalem because of their covenant unfaithfulness. Ezekiel as the "son of man," in many ways foreshadowed the ministry of Jesus. His message was directed specifically to Israel, and in Ezekiel 5:15 it is also made clear that Israel's judgment would, although not specifically directed towards the nations, serve as "a reproach, a taunt, a lesson, and an astonishment to the nations that are all around you, when I execute judgments among you (Israel) in anger and in fury and in furious rebukes."

To read through chapters 5-7 of Ezekiel is almost overwhelming with respect to its expression of God's fury against Jerusalem. There is so much in this extended passage that foreshadows and even directly points to much that is found in the book of Revelation, which according to one modern writer, "refers to a scenario that is described in horrific and heart-shaking detail in the single scariest book in all of scripture" (*A History of the End of the World*, Jonathan Kirsch, p.1). These three chapters from Ezekiel certainly fit this description as well. It is not however, just the "horrific and heart-shaking detail" that draws these two passages together. Many of the images and themes found in Ezekiel's prophecy are primary to the message of Revelation.

95

I am including the entire text of these three chapters from Ezekiel for easy reference with hopes that the reader will read them and give due consideration to these important texts. Another text of critical importance that the reader should keep firmly in mind is the scathing message of Jesus recorded in Matthew 23. In this passage, Jesus presents His message in much the same manner as the Old Testament prophets. He produces a litany of charges against His enemies and then warns of certain judgment to come upon that 1st century generation of Jews.

The wrath of God against those who had played the harlot and committed a multitude of abominations is a central theme of both passages (Ezekiel 5-7 & Revelation 17-19). Revelation 15:1 reveals that in the seven last plagues which are contained in the seven bowls, *"the wrath of God is complete"*. Another way of saying this is that God's anger and fury would be spent (Ezekiel 5:13, 6:12, 7:8). The word translated as *spent* in these three verses in Ezekiel is the Hebrew word *kalah* which means: "1) to be complete, be at an end, 2) to be completed, be finished, 3) to be accomplished, be fulfilled, 4) to be spent, be used up"[3]

Therefore when God said, "Now upon you I will soon pour out My fury, and spend My anger upon you; I will judge you according to your ways, and I will repay you for all your abominations" (Ezekiel 7:8), He is likewise saying that in this soon coming judgment the wrath of God would be complete.

---

[3] The Old Testament Hebrew Lexicon, http://www.studylight.org/lex/heb/view.cgi?number=03615).

In Ezekiel, it is stated that the wrath of God was to come against Jerusalem to repay her for her sinful ways and for her abominations. "My eye will not spare, nor will I have pity; I will repay you according to your ways, and your abominations will be in your midst. Then you shall know that I am the Lord who strikes" (Ezekiel 7:9).

In Revelation God remembers Babylon's ("the mother of harlots and of the abominations of the earth") iniquities and in Revelation 18:6 promised to repay her double according to her works (reference God's promise to judge Israel in Jeremiah 16:17-18). In Ezekiel 7:8, God used the imagery of pouring out His fury, while in Revelation 16 this image is somewhat magnified with a description of the seven bowls of wrath that would be poured out.

Seven times within Ezekiel chapters 5-7, the prophet proclaims that once God has poured out His fury upon Israel, "then they will know that I am the Lord" (Ezekiel 6: 7, 10, 13, 14; 7: 4, 9, 27). Likewise, at the judgment and destruction of Babylon, the one whose name is called *"The Word of God"* is revealed as the KING OF KINGS AND LORD OF LORDS (Revelation 19:16).

These are crucial and climactic images that are found in both passages (this theme is repeated many times over in Ezekiel's prophecy). In each passage, when God's wrath and fury have been fully poured out (spent, complete), this accomplished judgment proclaims the identity of the Lord. All throughout Ezekiel, and in a number of other Old Testament passages, it is through the judgment that He executes that the LORD is made known.

In the book of Revelation, it is through the judgment of Babylon that the identity of Jesus is unveiled. It is through this judgment of which He frequently had warned the rulers of Jerusalem during His earthly ministry, that Jesus would be manifested as the King of kings and LORD of lords. With this accomplished, all could now see that Jesus had indeed been exalted and was to be honored with the same honor as His Father (John 5:23).

Likewise no less than seven times in these three chapters of Ezekiel's prophecy, God made declarations through his prophet. "Thus says the Lord" (5:5, 6:11), "the word of the Lord came to me, saying" (6:1, 7:1), "'Therefore, as I live,' says the Lord GOD" (5:11), "I, the LORD, have spoken" (5:15,17). These phrases and others like them are repeated many times over throughout the prophetic writings of the Old Testament. God repeatedly made declarations through His prophets, but it was only as God fulfilled and brought to pass what He had declared that those in unbelief would know for certain that He was the LORD.

Ezekiel 5

"And you, son of man, take a sharp sword, take it as a barber's razor, and pass it over your head and your beard; then take scales to weigh and divide the hair. ²You shall burn with fire one-third in the midst of the city, when the days of the siege are finished; then you shall take one-third and strike around it with the sword, and one-third you shall scatter in the wind: I will draw out a sword after them. ³You shall also take a small number of them and bind them in the edge of your garment. ⁴Then take some of them again and throw them into the midst of the fire, and burn them in the fire. From there a fire will go out into all the house of Israel.

⁵ "Thus says the Lord God: 'This is Jerusalem; I have set her in the midst of the nations and the countries all around her. ⁶

She has rebelled against My judgments by doing wickedness more than the nations, and against My statutes more than the countries that are all around her; for they have refused My judgments, and they have not walked in My statutes.' [7] Therefore thus says the Lord God: 'Because you have multiplied disobedience more than the nations that are all around you, have not walked in My statutes nor kept My judgments, nor even done according to the judgments of the nations that are all around you'- [8] therefore thus says the Lord God: 'Indeed I, even I, am against you and will execute judgments in your midst in the sight of the nations. [9] And I will do among you what I have never done, and the like of which I will never do again, because of all your abominations. [10] Therefore fathers shall eat their sons in your midst, and sons shall eat their fathers; and I will execute judgments among you, and all of you who remain I will scatter to all the winds.

[11] 'Therefore, as I live,' says the Lord God, 'surely, because you have defiled My sanctuary with all your detestable things and with all your abominations, therefore I will also diminish you; My eye will not spare, nor will I have any pity. [12] One-third of you shall die of the pestilence, and be consumed with famine in your midst; and one-third shall fall by the sword all around you; and I will scatter another third to all the winds, and I will draw out a sword after them.

[13] 'Thus shall My anger be spent, and I will cause My fury to rest upon them, and I will be avenged; and they shall know that I, the Lord, have spoken it in My zeal, when I have spent My fury upon them. [14] Moreover I will make you a waste and

a reproach among the nations that are all around you, in the sight of all who pass by.

[15] 'So it shall be a reproach, a taunt, a lesson, and an astonishment to the nations that are all around you, when I execute judgments among you in anger and in fury and in furious rebukes. I, the Lord, have spoken. [16] When I send against them the terrible arrows of famine which shall be for destruction, which I will send to destroy you, I will increase the famine upon you and cut off your supply of bread. 17 So I will send against you famine and wild beasts, and they will bereave you. Pestilence and blood shall pass through you, and I will bring the sword against you. I, the Lord, have spoken.'"

Ezekiel 6

[1] Now the word of the Lord came to me, saying: [2] "Son of man, set your face toward the mountains of Israel, and prophesy against them, [3] and say, 'O mountains of Israel, hear the word of the Lord God! Thus says the Lord God to the mountains, to the hills, to the ravines, and to the valleys: "Indeed I, even I, will bring a sword against you, and I will destroy your high places. [4] Then your altars shall be desolate, your incense altars shall be broken, and I will cast down your slain men before your idols. [5] And I will lay the corpses of the children of Israel before their idols, and I will scatter your bones all around your altars. [6] In all your dwelling places the cities shall be laid waste, and the high places shall be desolate, so that your altars may be laid waste and made desolate, your idols may be broken and made to cease, your incense altars may be cut down, and your works may be abolished. [7] **The**

slain shall fall in your midst, and you shall know that I am the Lord.

[8] "Yet I will leave a remnant, so that you may have some who escape the sword among the nations, when you are scattered through the countries. [9] Then those of you who escape will remember Me among the nations where they are carried captive, because I was crushed by their adulterous heart which has departed from Me, and by their eyes which play the harlot after their idols; they will loathe themselves for the evils which they committed in all their abominations. [10] **And they shall know that I am the Lord**; I have not said in vain that I would bring this calamity upon them."

[11] 'Thus says the Lord God: "Pound your fists and stamp your feet, and say, 'Alas, for all the evil abominations of the house of Israel! For they shall fall by the sword, by famine, and by pestilence. [12] He who is far off shall die by the pestilence, he who is near shall fall by the sword, and he who remains and is besieged shall die by the famine. Thus will I spend My fury upon them. [13] **Then you shall know that I am the Lord**, when their slain are among their idols all around their altars, on every high hill, on all the mountaintops, under every green tree, and under every thick oak, wherever they offered sweet incense to all their idols. [14] So I will stretch out My hand against them and make the land desolate, yes, more desolate than the wilderness toward Diblah, in all their dwelling places. **Then they shall know that I am the Lord.**"'

Ezekiel 7

¹ Moreover the word of the Lord came to me, saying, ² "And you, son of man, thus says the Lord God to the land of Israel: 'An end! The end has come upon the four corners of the land. ³ Now the end has come upon you, and I will send My anger against you; I will judge you according to your ways, and I will repay you for all your abominations. ⁴ My eye will not spare you, nor will I have pity; but I will repay your ways, and your abominations will be in your midst; **then you shall know that I am the Lord!'** ⁵ "Thus says the Lord God: 'A disaster, a singular disaster; behold, it has come! ⁶ An end has come, the end has come; it has dawned for you; behold, it has come! ⁷ Doom has come to you, you who dwell in the land; the time has come, a day of trouble is near, and not of rejoicing in the mountains. ⁸ Now upon you I will soon pour out My fury, and spend My anger upon you; I will judge you according to your ways, and I will repay you for all your abominations. ⁹ 'My eye will not spare, nor will I have pity; I will repay you according to your ways, and your abominations will be in your midst. **Then you shall know that I am the Lord who strikes.**

¹⁰ 'Behold, the day! Behold, it has come! Doom has gone out; the rod has blossomed, pride has budded. ¹¹ Violence has risen up into a rod of wickedness; none of them shall remain, none of their multitude, none of them; nor shall there be wailing for them. ¹² The time has come, the day draws near. 'Let not the buyer rejoice, nor the seller mourn, for wrath is on their whole multitude. ¹³ For the seller shall not return to what has been sold, though he may still be alive; for the vision concerns the whole multitude, and it shall not turn back; no one will

strengthen himself who lives in iniquity. [14] 'They have blown the trumpet and made everyone ready, but no one goes to battle; for My wrath is on all their multitude. [15] The sword is outside, and the pestilence and famine within. Whoever is in the field will die by the sword; and whoever is in the city, famine and pestilence will devour him. [16] 'Those who survive will escape and be on the mountains like doves of the valleys, all of them mourning, each for his iniquity. [17] Every hand will be feeble, and every knee will be as weak as water. [18] They will also be girded with sackcloth; horror will cover them; shame will be on every face, baldness on all their heads. [19] 'They will throw their silver into the streets, and their gold will be like refuse; their silver and their gold will not be able to deliver them in the day of the wrath of the Lord; they will not satisfy their souls, nor fill their stomachs, because it became their stumbling block of iniquity. [20] 'As for the beauty of his ornaments, he set it in majesty; but they made from it the images of their abominations—their detestable things; therefore I have made it like refuse to them. [21] I will give it as plunder into the hands of strangers, and to the wicked of the earth as spoil; and they shall defile it. [22] I will turn My face from them, and they will defile My secret place; for robbers shall enter it and defile it. [23] 'Make a chain, for the land is filled with crimes of blood, and the city is full of violence. [24] Therefore I will bring the worst of the Gentiles, and they will possess their houses; I will cause the pomp of the strong to cease, and their holy places shall be defiled. [25] Destruction comes; they will seek peace, but there shall be none. [26] Disaster will come upon disaster, and rumor will be upon rumor. Then they will seek a vision from a prophet; but the law will perish from the priest, and counsel from the elders. [27] 'The king will mourn, the prince will be clothed with desolation, and the hands of the common people will tremble. I will do to them according to their way, and according to what they deserve I will judge them; **then they shall know that I am the Lord!**'"

It is not the intent here to perform a detailed study of these chapters. I would urge the reader to focus on how many times YHVH said that He was going to act in judgment and that as a direct result of His actions: "then they shall know that I am the Lord!"

I have given the full text of these chapters to help drive home this principle of God's identity being confirmed as He executes the judgment He had promised against His enemies. Although Jesus' message in Matthew 23 is a bit more concise, it is very similar in tone as His words display His anger just as God had displayed His through the awesome words in this portion of Ezekiel's prophecy. Simply note how chapter seven concludes: "I will judge them; then they shall know that I am the LORD" (Ezekiel 7:27). This brief statement is a wonderfully concise summary of the message and intent of Ezekiel 5-7.

This phrase ("then they (or you) shall know that I am the Lord") is found repeatedly in the Old Testament (in the writings of Ezekiel most frequently). The question that must be asked is how would "they" know that He was Lord (YHVH)? They (identity being context dependent, but would always be the ones targeted for judgment) would know this through the judgment and deliverance He executed upon and for the various peoples in the Old Testament days. Remember however the testimony of Ezekiel 5:15, and hear the words of Rahab when she spoke to the two men spying out Jericho. Word of God's judgment of the enemies of Israel had convinced the

104

people of Jericho that the God of Israel was truly "God in heaven above and on earth beneath."

> "Now before they lay down, she came up to them on the roof, and said to the men: 'I know that the LORD has given you the land, that the terror of you has fallen on us, and that all the inhabitants of the land are fainthearted because of you. For we have heard how the LORD dried up the water of the Red Sea for you when you came out of Egypt, and what you did to the two kings of the Amorites who were on the other side of the Jordan, Sihon and Og, whom you utterly destroyed. And as soon as we heard these things, our hearts melted; neither did there remain any more courage in anyone because of you, for the LORD your God, He is God in heaven above and on earth beneath'" (Joshua 2:8-11).

As God was in the process of fulfilling His promises to give Israel the land of Canaan, an interesting incident occurs involving the inhabitants of Gibeon. They had heard of the mighty works performed by the God of Israel. Rather than joining with the kings of the Hittites, the Amorites, the Canaanites, the Perizzites, the Hivites, and the Jebusites to fight against Joshua and Israel, they sought to deceive Joshua and the men of Israel in order to save themselves from the mighty hand of the Lord. "So they said to him: 'From a very far country your servants have come, because of the name of the LORD your God; for we have heard of His fame, and all that He did in Egypt, and all that He did to the two kings of the Amorites who were beyond the Jordan--to Sihon king of Heshbon, and Og king of Bashan, who was at Ashtaroth'" (Joshua 9:9- 10). None of these Old Testament people listed above had visibly seen God performing these

105

works and yet the Gibeonites recognized that "the arm of Lord" had certainly come against these people in a very real sense.

Having been almost continually rejected (especially by the religious leaders) during His earthly ministry and then finally crucified, Jesus repeatedly claimed that He would come in judgment against the generation who rejected and killed Him and His holy apostles. That is how He would prove, not only to the Jews, but to the whole world, that indeed: "Jesus Christ is Lord, to the glory of God the Father" (Philippians 2:11). It seems that the nature of sinful man is to ignore the source of God's great benefits, and only through God's terrible, but just judgments will they reluctantly acknowledge that God is Lord. Again, the Psalmist made it plain that this was true. "The Lord is known by the judgment He executes" (Psalm 9:16).

In the OT, God was never revealed as Lord by His visible presence. It is interesting to note in 1 Timothy that Paul spoke of, "our Lord Jesus Christ's appearing, which He will manifest in His own time, He who is the blessed and only Potentate, the King of kings and Lord of lords, who alone has immortality, dwelling in unapproachable light, whom no man has seen or can see" (1 Timothy 6:15-16). This future appearing to which Paul here referred would be a time at which Jesus would manifest Himself as one with God, whom no man has seen or can see. Jesus had demonstrated His humanity as Israel's Messiah while He walked upon the earth (see Matthew 11:2-5). His humanity was well established. It would not do for Him to return again in human form since that would not be a demonstration of His divinity, nor would it demonstrate that God had exalted him and given Him a name above every name. As Don Preston is fond of saying: "Jesus was not going to be revealed, again, as a 5' 5" Jewish man, but, as King of kings and Lord of lords!"

106

Certainly there have been many down through the years who acknowledged Jesus historically as a "good man" yet denied His equality with God. Even some professing to believe in Jesus Christ have denied his divinity and in doing so would seem to bring into question the efficacy of Christ's sacrifice. Could the sacrifice of a mere man be sufficient to take away the sins of the world? Jesus' 1st century enemies would never have denied His humanity. The pinch came with Jesus' claim to be one with God. His confrontation with Caiaphas and the Sanhedrin revolved around Jesus' claim to be the Son of God. Their refusal to believe this assertion, elicited a response from Jesus that they (1st century people) would see Him coming on clouds of heaven (Matthew 26:64), clearly a reference to divine judgment. Jesus was in essence telling them that He would soon come in judgment as the Father had in times past. This would prove the truthfulness of His claim that He was the Son of God to whom the Father had committed all judgment (John 5:22). Because they understood what Jesus' words implied, the council answered Caiaphas and said: "He is deserving of death" (Matthew 26:66).

Many today recognize that Jesus was an actual historical person (in fact few even in the academic world deny that Jesus lived and died in the 1st century) and yet the modern church typically forfeits what is certainly its greatest apologetic argument to demonstrate the divine identity of the One whose name it proclaims as Lord.

Early Christians accepted Jesus as the Son of God. It was not to them that Jesus directed His boldest claims and threats of coming judgment. There had been others noted in both the Old Testament and New Testament writings that were reported to have been raised from the dead; therefore His resurrection did not in itself differentiate Jesus from these others and "prove" that He was the Son of God.

In Philippians 2:9, Paul stated that God had exalted Jesus, and in Romans 1:4 he said that Jesus was declared to be Son of God by His resurrection from the dead. This declaration was foundational to Paul's ministry, but there had at that time been no demonstration, no action to positively back up and establish the validity of this declaration.

Jesus claimed to be the Son of God (Matthew 26:62-64; Luke 22:70; John 9:35-37; John 11:4); the angel told Mary that her son would be called the Son of God (Luke 1:35); God Himself identified Jesus as His beloved Son (Matthew 3:17, 17:5; Mark 1:11, 9:7; Luke 3:22, 9:35), and Mark (Mark 1:1), Paul (Romans 1:4; 2 Corinthians 1:19; Hebrews 4:14; Acts 9:20), and John (John 1:34, 20:31; 1 John 4:15, 5:5) declared that He was the Son of God. Even the demons (Matthew 8:28-29; Mark 3:1) and unclean spirits (Luke 4:41) recognized Him as the Son of God. The declaration had been made many times over in the New Testament, but as was the pattern in the Old Testament, a subsequent demonstration would follow the declaration in order to vindicate its truthfulness. Multiple times Jesus had stated that He (not the Father) would come in judgment and as the Father had done in previous times, Jesus' coming in judgment would vindicate His own claims, as well as the declarations of God and the inspired Apostles.

Was it therefore necessary that Jesus come in a visible, bodily form, perhaps riding on a white horse or visibly riding on the clouds, as "literal" readings of certain New Testament passages would require, in order for him to come in judgment as the Father had come in Old Testament times? A thorough examination of the Old Covenant scriptures would suggest otherwise. The prophets describe in much detail how God typically judged a disobedient people.

108

The prophecies of Jeremiah and Ezekiel are filled with statements attributed to God that contain promises that He would "send the sword upon them", "send the sword after them", "draw out a sword after them", "bring the sword against them", "bring a sword on that land", "pursue them with the sword", "brandish My sword before them", "draw My sword out of its sheath;" promises which if taken "literally" would require that God was to physically appear with sword in hand chasing down those He had promised to judge.

It may well be that one significant barrier to a proper understanding of New Testament eschatological passages, is a lack of familiarity with the language and methods used by God in the Hebrew Scriptures. This should not be true of the scholarly within the church, but there is no doubt that many within today's church have at most only a superficial familiarity with much of the Old Testament. Some churches or denominations that claim to be "New Covenant churches," proudly proclaim their lack of interest in the Old Testament scriptures. Even those today who do attempt to seriously study these ancient scriptures, most likely have nothing approaching the level of knowledge of these texts possessed by many of those to whom the New Testament documents were addressed.

For some there also appears to be a tendency to dichotomize between the Old and New Testaments as pertains to how certain texts are to be understood. While recognizing that there is much use of apocalyptic, figurative and perhaps metaphoric language in the Old Testament, they inexplicably understand similar language found in the New Testament in a more literalistic manner, as if there had been a fundamental change in the type of literary styles used by the New Testament writers in contrast to the Old. Rather than recognize that these 1st century writers were grounded in the old Hebraic literary styles in which their contemporary culture was steeped, many insist on a "straightforward," "literal" reading of these 1st century writings.

Having looked at this extended passage from the early part of Ezekiel's prophecy that promised judgment for covenant disobedience, perhaps it would be a helpful exercise to examine how the Old Covenant prophets portrayed the accomplishment of this judgment.

The great prophets Ezekiel and Jeremiah were contemporaries who prophesied of and lived through the Babylonian captivity with its accompanying destruction of the city of Jerusalem and its temple. Both foretold how God would pour out His wrath against the southern kingdom of Judah.

As noted both of these prophets dealt extensively with the coming Babylonian invasion which would bring about the destruction of the city and temple along with the deportation of the bulk of the Jewish people living in the region of Judea. It is clear that God was promising to bring this judgment to pass, but the critical question for this discussion is: how would this judgment be accomplished?

"And the Lord has sent to you all His servants the prophets, rising early and sending them, but you have not listened nor inclined your ear to hear. They said, 'Repent now everyone of his evil way and his evil doings, and dwell in the land that the Lord has given to you and your fathers forever and ever. Do not go after other gods to serve them and worship them, and do not provoke Me to anger with the works of your hands; and I will not harm you.' Yet you have not listened to Me," says the Lord, "that you might provoke Me to anger with the works

110

of your hands to your own hurt. "Therefore thus says the Lord of hosts: 'Because you have not heard My words, behold, I will send and take all the families of the north,' says the Lord, 'and Nebuchadnezzar the king of Babylon, My servant, and will bring them against this land, against its inhabitants, and against these nations all around, and will utterly destroy them, and make them an astonishment, a hissing, and perpetual desolations" (Jeremiah 25:4-9).

In this passage Nebuchadnezzar who was the king of Babylon, is identified as God's servant. This is confirmed or reaffirmed later in Jeremiah 27:6 and Jeremiah 43:10. In what sense was he God's servant? Just as is seen above, a number of Old Testament passages (Revelation 10:7 as well) speak of the prophets as God's servants, but it is obvious that Nebuchadnezzar doesn't fit there. Abraham, Moses, and David (among several others) are frequently referred to by God as "My servant". These men clearly were, despite their flaws, some of the godliest men presented to us in the scriptures, but in contrast what the Old Testament portrays in the case of Nebuchadnezzar is a picture of one in whose hand God placed His sword of judgment.

When God spoke of "the sword I will send among them," He was pointing to Nebuchadnezzar who would be the instrument through whom He would pour out His wrath. In a very real sense, Nebuchadnezzar was himself God's sword of wrath. All of these events took place in an even larger context of the expansion of the Babylonian Empire. Judea was not the only target of Nebuchadnezzar's aggression. There are passages in their prophesies in which Jeremiah and Ezekiel are again in agreement as they focus on God's judgment of Egypt in light of the long (mostly negative) history of their relationship with Israel, which had continued even up

111

to that present time. Ezekiel's prophecy against Egypt gives great light to much of what is being discussed here.

"I will strengthen the arms of the king of Babylon and put My sword in his hand; but I will break Pharaoh's arms, and he will groan before him with the groanings of a mortally wounded man. Thus I will strengthen the arms of the king of Babylon, but the arms of Pharaoh shall fall down; they shall know that I am the Lord, **when I put My sword into the hand of the king of Babylon** and he stretches it out against the land of Egypt. I will scatter the Egyptians among the nations and disperse them throughout the countries. Then they shall know that I am the Lord'" (Ezekiel 30:24-26).

"'I will also trouble the hearts of many peoples, when I bring your destruction among the nations, into the countries which you have not known. Yes, I will make many peoples astonished at you, and their kings shall be horribly afraid of you when I brandish My sword before them; and they shall tremble every moment, every man for his own life, in the day of your fall. 'For thus says the Lord God: "The sword of the king of Babylon shall come upon you. By the swords of the mighty warriors, all of them the most terrible of the nations, I will cause your multitude to fall. "They shall plunder the pomp of Egypt, and all its multitude shall be destroyed. also I will destroy all its animals from beside its great waters; the foot of man shall muddy them no more, nor shall the hooves of animals muddy them. Then I will make their waters clear, and make their rivers run like oil," says the Lord God. "When I make the land of Egypt desolate, and the country is destitute

112

of all that once filled it, when I strike all who dwell in it, then they shall know that I am the Lord" (Ezekiel 32:9-16).

In Ezekiel chapter 30, God spoke of putting His sword in the hand of the king of Babylon, while in chapter 32 He essentially equates His sword with that of the king of Babylon. Here God said that when He put His sword into the hand of the king, and when the swords of the mighty warriors who were following the command of the king make the land of Egypt desolate, then the Egyptians would know that He is the Lord. It was not through His own immediate actions, but through those of the Chaldean army as God strengthened the arms of the king. The text clearly proclaims that the king of Babylon would stretch out God's sword against the land of Egypt. This is language that cannot be taken in a literalistic manner and it demands that the reader acknowledge the figurative nature of the prophet's words. This is the only way that it can be properly understood.

As was noted earlier, Jeremiah lived through the Babylonia conquest of the southern kingdom of Judah. In the book of Lamentations, Jeremiah in fact gave a fascinating account of God's judgment, his own resulting despondency, and ultimately God's merciful consolation for His faithful servants. His description in chapter 2 is striking in its attribution to God of all the destruction that Nebuchadnezzar and his armies had brought down upon Jerusalem.

"How the Lord has covered the daughter of Zion with a cloud in His anger! He cast down from heaven to the earth the beauty of Israel, and did not remember His footstool in the day of His anger. The Lord has swallowed up and has not pitied all the dwelling places of Jacob. He has thrown down in His wrath the strongholds of the daughter of Judah;

113

He has brought them down to the ground; He has profaned the kingdom and its princes. He has cut off in fierce anger every horn of Israel; He has drawn back His right hand from before the enemy. He has blazed against Jacob like a flaming fire devouring all around. Standing like an enemy, He has bent His bow; with His right hand, like an adversary, He has slain all who were pleasing to His eye; on the tent of the daughter of Zion, He has poured out His fury like fire. The Lord was like an enemy. He has swallowed up Israel, He has swallowed up all her palaces; He has destroyed her strongholds, and has increased mourning and lamentation in the daughter of Judah. He has done violence to His tabernacle, as if it were a garden; He has destroyed His place of assembly; the Lord has caused the appointed feasts and Sabbaths to be forgotten in Zion. In His burning indignation He has spurned the king and the priest... The Lord has done what He purposed; He has fulfilled His word which He commanded in days of old. He has thrown down and has not pitied, and He has caused an enemy to rejoice over you; He has exalted the horn of your adversaries" (Lamentations 2:1-6, 17).

Note how emphatically Jeremiah proclaimed the actions of the Lord. Repeatedly the prophet stated in reference to God, "He has..." as he described the actions of God in pouring out His wrath. He then concludes the chapter with this bold claim: "The LORD has done what He purposed; He has fulfilled His word which He commanded in days of old." There is also the terrible image in verse 3 of God drawing back His protective hand so as to allow the Babylonians to come against the daughter of Zion.

114

A consistently literal reading of this passage would lead one to believe that it was God Himself who had been physically present and that He had in actuality and in a "literal" manner, "bent His bow; with His right hand, like an adversary." Yet, what person having read the entire context of Jeremiah and Ezekiel in the prophecies discussed here, would deny that Nebuchadnezzar and his army were the actual instruments of God's judgment? And yet it was God who was the ultimate cause behind these events. But I would also assert that God was the mediate cause. He was the indirect cause in the sense that He was acting through the intervening agency of the Babylonia king. This does not diminish the glory of God; rather it magnifies His power as it demonstrates His control over, and His providential use of even heathen nations to bring about fulfillment of His purposes.

This episode is not the only example that could be described, but it is probably the most thoroughly documented and discussed within the Old Testament survey of God's dealings with Israel. It gives the reader the best picture of how God has typically manifested, or brought to pass His judgment within a historical framework.

We will also consider briefly the judgment of the northern kingdom of Israel described in 1 Kings 17. Beginning in verse 5, the writer detailed how Israel was carried away to Assyria: "Now the king of Assyria went throughout all the land, and went up to Samaria and besieged it for three years. In the ninth year of Hoshea, the king of Assyria took Samaria and carried Israel away to Assyria, and placed them in Halah and by the Habor, the River of Gozan, and in the cities of the Medes" (1 Kings 17:5-6). In the 11 verses that follow, the writer catalogued how "Israel had sinned against the Lord their God", and then concluded with this final statement: "Therefore the Lord was very angry with Israel, and removed them from His sight; there was none left but the tribe of Judah alone" (1 Kings 17:18). Verse 18

115

explicitly states that it was the Lord Who removed Israel from His sight, and yet verse 6 asserts that it was the king of Assyria who carried Israel away. If we adhere here to a strict literalism, we have a contradiction, but if we follow what has been seen and understood regarding God's judgment of Judah there is really no difficulty in grasping how God accomplished the judgment of His enemies (who in this instance were the 10 northern tribes of Israel).

As we look closely at passages such as the ones we have examined above, our understanding of how God chose to share the unfolding of these events should be greatly enhanced, and when confronted with similar language and circumstances in later passages of scripture, we should be better prepared to understand the message presented to God's 1st century people.

Jesus' statements claiming to be the Son of God, and in some sense equal with God, were obviously made in the presence of 1st century Jews. These Jews were also the ones who first rejected these claims. It was to this 1st century generation of Jews as well, that Jesus proclaimed that he as the Son of Man, would come in judgment before that generation passed away. The events that would vindicate His claims, were to be in response to their rejection and crucifixion of Him *and* their subsequent actions against Jesus' disciples as they filled up the measure of sin (Matthew 23:32). If this judgment did not occur before the eyes of that Jewish generation, the evidentiary value of that event to that generation, and thus the manifestation and demonstration of Jesus' oneness with God the Father, was non-existent.

When Jesus told Caiaphas and the Sanhedrin, "Hereafter you will see the Son of Man sitting at the right hand of the Power, and coming on the clouds of heaven" (Matthew 26:64), His words were meaningless

116

posturing, or worse, if He did not fulfill them before all those to whom He spoke had died - in other words, within that 1st century generation. Although not using the exact phraseology so frequently found in the Old Testament, Jesus was in essence saying, "Then you will know that I am the LORD." They would know that God had indeed "exalted Him and given Him the name which is above every name" (Philippians 2:9).

Jesus told the scribes and Pharisees in Matthew 23, and Caiaphas and the Sanhedrin in Matthew 26, that He would come in judgment against them. The destruction that came upon Jerusalem and its temple in 70AD was seen by many early Christians as fulfillment of this warning. It fit the pattern established in the Old Testament and was used as a powerful apologetic during the first centuries of the church. Unfortunately (at least in my view) the modern church has for the most part departed from a message proclaiming Jesus' faithful fulfillment of His words to a message of indefinite postponement.

117

Conclusion

It was generally through His actions within history, in response to His stated promises, that God revealed Himself. Amos 3:7 supplies a very important and interesting statement. "Surely the Lord God does nothing, unless He reveals His secret to His servants the prophets." Based on this passage, one can see that God's primary method was to reveal His formerly secret intentions to His prophets who would then proclaim it to the people of Israel (or others as God directed). When God faithfully performed that which He promised, they would then know for certain that He was indeed the Lord of Heaven.

The primary way that God differentiated between Himself as God and the other so-called 'gods' in Old Testament times, was by declaring beforehand what He would do and then bringing it to pass. In Isaiah 41, God belittled those who made idols for themselves, and in verses 21-26 issued the following challenge to those who would follow after other gods.

"'Present your case,' says the Lord. 'Bring forth your strong reasons,' says the King of Jacob. 'Let them bring forth and show us what will happen; let them show the former things, what they were, that we may consider them, and know the latter end of them; or declare to us things to come. Show the things that are to come hereafter, that we may know that you are gods; yes, do good or do evil, that we may be dismayed and see it together. Indeed you are nothing, and your work is nothing; he who chooses you is an abomination. 'I have raised up one from the north, and he shall come; from the rising of the sun he shall call on My name; and he shall come against princes as though mortar, as the potter treads clay. Who has

118

declared from the beginning, that we may know? And former times, that we may say, 'He is righteous'? Surely there is no one who shows, surely there is no one who declares, surely there is no one who hears your words.'"

In chapter 46:5-11 the prophet proclaimed a very similar message:

"To whom will you liken Me, and make Me equal and compare Me, that we should be alike? They lavish gold out of the bag, and weigh silver on the scales; they hire a goldsmith, and he makes it a god; they prostrate themselves, yes, they worship. They bear it on the shoulder, they carry it and set it in its place, and it stands; from its place it shall not move. Though one cries out to it, yet it cannot answer nor save him out of his trouble. 'Remember this, and show yourselves men; recall to mind, O you transgressors. Remember the former things of old, for I am God, and there is no other; I am God, and there is none like Me, declaring the end from the beginning, and from ancient times things that are not yet done, saying, 'My counsel shall stand, and I will do all My pleasure,' calling a bird of prey from the east, the man who executes My counsel, from a far country. Indeed I have spoken it; I will also bring it to pass. I have purposed it; I will also do it.'"

This is precisely what Jesus did! He spoke it as the prophet like Moses (Acts 3:22; Deuteronomy 18:15), and He brought it to pass just as YHVH had done multiple times in the days of old, as the Father gave Him the power of judgment (John 5:22)! This was done so "that all should honor the Son just as they honor the Father" (John 5:23). As was said so often of YHVH by the prophets of Old, then

119

they would know that Jesus was Lord. I would hope that anyone would be very cautious of denying this truth.

The following comments on Matthew 24:30 ("And then shall appear the sign of the Son of man") by the great English Biblical critic and Hebraist John Lightfoot is an appropriate way to help bring this discussion to a close:

> "Then shall **the Son of man** give a proof of himself, who they would not before acknowledge: a proof, indeed, not in any visible figure, but in vengeance and judgment so visible, that all the tribes of the earth shall be forced to acknowledge him the avenger. The Jews would not know him: now they shall know him, whether they will or no, Isa. xxvi. II (*"Lord, when Your hand is lifted up, they will not see. But they will see and be ashamed for their envy of people; yes, the fire of Your enemies shall devour them")*. Many times they asked of him a **sign**: now a **sign** shall appear, that he is the true Messiah, whom they despised, derided, and crucified, namely, his signal vengeance and fury, such as never any nation felt from the first foundations of the world" *(A Commentary on the New Testament from the Talmud and Hebraica,,* vol. 2, p. 320, A total 6 volumes were published from 1658-1678).

Lightfoot's comments pertain more directly to Jesus' status as Messiah and this is certainly of great importance, but even more critical is the vindication of His claim to be one with God; to be the unique Son of God; to be *LORD!*

120

In Luke 17, Jesus pointed to the imminent coming of the kingdom of God. He associated the coming of the kingdom with the judgment of those who would reject and ultimately crucify Him. He likened this judgment to that which came upon the land in the days of Noah, and said that this would be the "day when the Son of Man is revealed" (v.30). The Son of Man would be revealed through the promised judgment of those who murdered Him.

Apokalupto: "1. to uncover, lay open what has been veiled or covered up a. disclose, make bare, 2. to make known, make manifest, disclose what before was unknown" (The KJV New Testament Greek Lexicon). The use of this word by Jesus indicated the He realized that His earthly ministry had not fully revealed His complete and full identity. The coming judgment would "disclose what before was unknown": "that Jesus Christ was Lord, to the glory of God the Father." The judgment that He would bring in the Father's name against Old Covenant Jerusalem revealed Jesus to be the Son of God and would bear witness to those who did not believe. "Jesus answered them, 'I told you, and you do not believe. The works that I do in My Father's name, they bear witness of Me'" (John 10:25).

Paul used this same Greek word (*Apokalupto*) in his second letter to the Thessalonians. It was used again in the context of the imminent judgment of those who were persecuting those 1st century Christians, who did not know God and who did not obey the gospel of Jesus Christ. Taken in its proper context, this text was addressing contemporary issues and was not speaking generically of the judgment of all unbelievers in all ages. Jesus would be revealed (Strong's Concordance gives this on the Greek work transliterated as *apokalypsis*: "used of events by which things or states or persons hitherto withdrawn from view are made visible to all") as Lord

121

through the events of the 1st century judgment of those who were persecuting the Christians.

> "We are bound to thank God always for you, brethren, as it is fitting, because your faith grows exceedingly, and the love of every one of you all abounds toward each other, so that we ourselves boast of you among the churches of God for your patience and faith in all your persecutions and tribulations that you endure, which is manifest evidence of the righteous judgment of God, that you may be counted worthy of the kingdom of God, for which you also suffer; since it is a righteous thing with God to repay with tribulation those who trouble you, and to give you who are troubled rest with us when the Lord Jesus is revealed from heaven with His mighty angels, in flaming fire taking vengeance on those who do not know God, and on those who do not obey the gospel of our Lord Jesus Christ" (2 Thessalonians 1:3-8).

Some have commented that what took place in Judea would have no real impact on the circumstances of those living in various other places, such as Thessalonica, throughout the Roman Empire. It is important to understand that this conflict actually had a much broader scope and was not simply limited to the immediate Judean area. Josephus in his *War of the Jews* provides historical detail for the breadth of the Roman war, supporting the notion that others outside of the Palestine area were significantly impacted by this conflict.

In short, Jesus promised to come in judgment. He said that the Father had given Him the prerogative of judgment and that in exercising this prerogative, He would be honored as the Father was honored. Jesus the Christ, in fulfilling the promised judgment of Judah and

Jerusalem, fully revealed Himself as the Son of God. This is an incredibly important concept that is recognized by too few Christians today. It is the truth that should answer to, and shut the mouth of, the skeptics and enemies of Christianity. Those Christians who deny, or simply do not recognize the importance of the events circa 70AD, play right into the hands of these critics. At the same time, they unintentionally demean the name of their Lord and King. Were we as His people more diligent to try to understand these things, we would be equipped to stand up and boldly proclaim the amazing fulfillment of Jesus' words as manifested in the destruction and judgment of Old Covenant Jerusalem, then certainly many skeptics would be challenged anew to reconsider the truth claims of Christianity.

Lest it be charged that our focus is exclusive to the judgment of Old Covenant Judaism, let us remember the claims of the apostle Paul that in Christ "we have redemption through His blood, the forgiveness of sins, according to the riches of His grace" (Ephesians 1:7). As is seen in many similar statements in the New Testament, Jesus is here essentially assigned a position previously attributed in the Old Testament scriptures solely to the LORD, the "Holy One of Israel". As the psalmist said, "O Israel, hope in the Lord; for with the Lord there is mercy, and with Him is abundant redemption" (Psalm 130:7). In Luke's gospel, Anna the prophetess identified the child Jesus as Israel's redeemer and "spoke of Him to all those who looked for redemption in Jerusalem" (Luke 2:38). That redemption and Jesus' vindication as Israel's redeemer would not, as Luke makes clear, be fully accomplished until He came in judgment against the old earthly Jerusalem: "But when you see Jerusalem surrounded by armies, then know that its desolation is near. . . Then they will see the Son of Man coming in a cloud with power and great glory. Now when these things begin to happen, look up and lift up your heads, because your redemption draws near" (Luke 21:20, 27-28).

123

The climax of it all is proclaimed in the book Revelation and as we allow the word of God speak for itself (Keeping in mind Revelation 1:1 and 20:6), we conclude with these glorious words:

"And I saw in the right hand of Him who sat on the throne a scroll written inside and on the back, sealed with seven seals. [2] Then I saw a strong angel proclaiming with a loud voice, "Who is worthy to open the scroll and to loose its seals?" [3] And no one in heaven or on the earth or under the earth was able to open the scroll, or to look at it.

[4] So I wept much, because no one was found worthy to open and read the scroll, or to look at it. [5] But one of the elders said to me, "Do not weep. Behold, the Lion of the tribe of Judah, the Root of David, has prevailed to open the scroll and to loose its seven seals."

[6] And I looked, and behold, in the midst of the throne and of the four living creatures, and in the midst of the elders, stood a Lamb as though it had been slain, having seven horns and seven eyes, which are the seven Spirits of God sent out into all the earth. [7] Then He came and took the scroll out of the right hand of Him who sat on the throne.

[8] Now when He had taken the scroll, the four living creatures and the twenty-four elders fell down before the Lamb, each having a harp, and golden bowls full of incense, which are the prayers of the saints. [9] And they sang a new song, saying:

"You are worthy to take the scroll, and to open its seals; for You were slain, and have redeemed us to

God by Your blood out of every tribe and tongue
and people and nation, [10]and have made us
kings and priests to our God; and we
shall reign on the earth."

[11] Then I looked, and I heard the voice of many angels around
the throne, the living creatures, and the elders; and the number
of them was ten thousand times ten thousand, and thousands
of thousands, [12] saying with a loud voice:

"Worthy is the Lamb who was slain
to receive power and riches and wisdom,
and strength and honor and glory and blessing!"
[13]And every creature which is in heaven and on the earth and
under the earth and such as are in the sea, and all that are in
them, I heard saying:
"Blessing and honor and glory and power be to Him
who sits on the throne, and to the Lamb,
forever and ever!"
[15] Then the four living creatures said, "Amen!" And the
twenty-four elders fell down and worshiped Him who lives
forever and ever." (Revelation 5)

It is very clear in this passage that the Lamb, who is described as the
Lion of the tribe of Judah and as the Root of David (both images that
point back to Jesus' earthly incarnation) was, because of God's
declarations, worthy to receive blessings and honor and glory and
power, just as the One who sits on the throne (the Father). The
Lamb's identity however, was still somewhat of a mystery, and it is
not until Jesus would take on the prerogative of judgment that the

Father had given to Him (John 5:21-23), that His identity would be fully revealed:

> "Now I saw heaven opened, and behold, a white horse. And He who sat on him was called Faithful and True, and in righteousness He judges and makes war. His eyes were like a flame of fire, and on His head were many crowns. He had a name written that no one knew except Himself. He was clothed with a robe dipped in blood, and His name is called The Word of God. And the armies in heaven, clothed in fine linen, white and clean, followed Him on white horses. Now out of His mouth goes a sharp sword, that with it He should strike the nations. And He Himself will rule them with a rod of iron. He Himself treads the winepress of the fierceness and wrath of Almighty God. And He has on His robe and on His thigh a name written:

KING OF KINGS AND
LORD OF LORDS.
(Revelation 19:11-16)

"Therefore God also has highly exalted Him and given Him the name which is above every name,that at the name of Jesus every knee should bow, of those in heaven, and of those on earth, and of those under the earth, and that every tongue should confess that Jesus Christ is Lord, to the glory of God the Father"
(Philippians 2:9-11)

Amen!

126

Appendix

Below you will find the text of a letter that I recently wrote to address some uncertainty found in the mind of a dear friend of mine over how the covenant curses found in the Old Testament relate to modern day Israel and their future, or possibly to their struggle down through the historical past. He is firmly futurist in his eschatological views and these are some thoughts that I pulled together that I hoped would bring some clarity to that particular conundrum and possibly some other closely related issues. My hope is that this relatively short excursus will benefit the reader of this work as well and shed some light with regard to the centrality of God's covenantal dealings with Israel as the primary, if not the exclusive, focus of the documents that make up our Bible.

I appreciate your candor in acknowledging the difficulty and uncertainty you have had in reconciling the promised judgment in passages such as Leviticus 26 and Deuteronomy 28 with how they would be or were worked out in the history of Israel. I doubt if the majority of modern Christians struggle with this issue as you have because very few of them are likely as serious in their studies of the Bible as you are. Although I made the comment that I didn't think that things were as complicated as they seemed to you, it was not always as clear to me as I see it today. For many years I was aware of these passages, but gave them little serious thought. In more recent years I have begun to see how important they are and also how so many other passages are tied to them either directly or indirectly.

Many Christians spend little time in study of the Old Testament and even if they do, generally fail to see the significance of these passages, which I believe are reiterated or built upon repeatedly in the prophetic writings that follow throughout the Old Testament. The constant warnings found in the prophets must be, and I believe can only be properly understood in light of the context of Leviticus 26 and Deuteronomy 28. Without a doubt these are two immensely important passages and ignorance of them makes it difficult, if not impossible to properly interpret and understand almost all the scriptures that follow. That includes the New Testament as well as the Old.

A critical verse that seems to be little noticed is Leviticus 26:25 where God said to Israel: "And I will bring a sword against you that will execute the vengeance of the covenant; when you are gathered together within your cities I will send pestilence among you, and you shall be delivered into the hands of the enemy." Note in particular the phrase, *"the vengeance of the covenant."* This phrase embodies a concept that is fundamental to understanding numerous passages, but I want to look at one in particular that is to me uniquely important.

Luke 21:20-22 is a passage that I believe ties directly to Leviticus 26:25 (really to the whole of Leviticus 26). In verse 22, Jesus said: "For these are the days of vengeance, that all things which are written may be fulfilled." It seems to me very clear that Jesus was saying that they were or would shortly be living in the "days of vengeance," and it was for the purpose "that all things which are written may be fulfilled." How did Jesus mean for this statement to be understood? Is "all things which are written," to be understood as inclusive of all the prophetic writings? I suppose that is subject to question, but surely it includes the "vengeance of the covenant" spoken of in Leviticus 26:25 and would also be inclusive of all passages that deal with God's promised vengeance toward covenant disobedience as expressed in Leviticus 26, Deuteronomy 28 and numerous other Old Testament prophetic passages.

As He talked directly to His disciples, Jesus began this section by saying: "But when you see Jerusalem surrounded by armies, then know that its desolation is near" (Luke 21:20). Jesus clearly stated (by using the personal pronoun "you" in reference to those to whom He spoke) that at least some of His 1st century disciples would see this take place. When they (His 1st century disciples) saw Jerusalem surrounded by armies, they would know that the days of covenant vengeance had arrived. A few verses later, Jesus again reemphasized the imminence of what He was pointing to: "Assuredly, I say to you, this generation will by no means pass away till these things take place" (Luke 21:32). Many see this as a difficult passage and yet to me it is one of the clearest statements that Jesus ever made.

If one looks closely at the three parallel passages of Matthew 24, Mark 13, and Luke 21, it should be very easy to see that Jesus was speaking specifically to His contemporary disciples with the clear expectation that they would be the ones to see those things come to pass. He used the personal pronouns "you" and "your" 25 times in Luke, 20 times in Mark and 18 times in Matthew, so it should be quite obvious that He was talking specifically to people of His generation.

The events that took place in relation to the destruction of Jerusalem in 70AD are given little if any significance in the mind of many, many modern Christians and yet I believe that they are fundamental to understanding a multitude of prophetic passages found throughout the scriptures.

Familiarity with the Old Testament scriptures should prepare one to see that the Old (or Mosaic) Covenant was never intended by God to be permanent. It had a distinct purpose, but in order for God to make a new covenant with Israel, the Old would of necessity have to be

130

fulfilled and then pass away. A major part of that fulfillment would be the ultimate promised judgment (or vengeance) that would come against Old Covenant Israel for not being "careful to do all his commandments and his statutes that I command you" (Deuteronomy 28:15).

In Leviticus 26:14-16, God very plainly said: "But if you will not listen to me and will not do all these commandments, [15] if you spurn my statutes, and if your soul abhors my rules, so that you will not do all my commandments, but break my covenant, [16] then I will do this to you:" He then proceeded to list in detail the consequences of their disobedience. For God to be faithful and true to the terms of the covenant, He must fulfill this promise of judgment if the behavior of His covenant people demanded it. This I firmly believe He did in 70AD.

That the new covenant would be different from the Old, and that the Old would ultimately pass away, was made plain in Chapters 30 and 31 of Jeremiah's prophecy. Here he spoke of restoring Judah and Israel, but it would not be as they had been before they were sent into exile. It was to be a faithful remnant that would be restored (Jeremiah 31:7), just as Isaiah had repeatedly prophesied (see Isaiah 10:20-22; 11:10-16). This is the context of God's marvelous promise of a new covenant with the house of Israel and the house of Judah found in Jeremiah 31:31-34.

> "Behold, the days are coming, says the LORD, when I will make a new covenant with the house of Israel and with the house of Judah- not according to the covenant that I made with their fathers in the day that I took them by the hand to lead them out of the land of Egypt, My covenant which they broke, though I was a husband to them, says the Lord. But this

is the covenant that I will make with the house of Israel after those days, says the Lord: I will put My law in their minds, and write it on their hearts; and I will be their God, and they shall be My people. No more shall every man teach his neighbor, and every man his brother, saying, 'Know the Lord,' for they all shall know Me, from the least of them to the greatest of them, says the LORD. For I will forgive their iniquity, and their sin I will remember no more" (Jeremiah 31:31-34).

Another related prophecy of great importance is Isaiah 49 which spoke of a raising up/restoration of Israel (Israel and Judah), and pointed to the fact that the Servant of God (Jesus Christ) would Himself be given as a covenant to the people. It is also stated here that it was too small a thing that God would restore Israel - the Servant would also be given as a light to the Gentiles. Here we see that although this covenant was promised to Israel as a whole, it would also incorporate the Gentiles into the one covenantal people of God. It pointed to fulfillment of God's promise to Abraham that in him, "all the families of the earth shall be blessed" (Genesis 12:5, see also Acts 3:25). Here are what I see as the most critical verses from Isaiah 49 (not to say that the entire passage is not very important):

"And now the LORD says, Who formed Me from the womb to be His Servant, to bring Jacob back to Him, so that Israel is gathered to Him (For I shall be glorious in the eyes of the LORD, and My God shall be My strength), [6] indeed He says, 'It is too small a thing that You should be My Servant to raise up the tribes of Jacob, and to restore the preserved ones of Israel; I will also give You as a light to the Gentiles, that You should be My salvation to the ends of the earth.'"

132

⁶ Thus says the Lord, the Redeemer of Israel, their Holy One, to Him whom man despises, to Him whom the nation abhors, to the Servant of rulers: "Kings shall see and arise, princes also shall worship, because of the LORD who is faithful, the Holy One of Israel; and He has chosen You." ⁸ "Thus says the LORD: "In an acceptable time I have heard You, and in the day of salvation I have helped You; I will preserve You and give You as a covenant to the people, to restore the earth, to cause them to inherit the desolate heritages" (Isaiah 49:5-8).

The fact that Paul quoted from this passage in his second letter to the church at Corinth, as well as the fact that he forcefully stated: *"Behold, now is the accepted time; behold, now is the day of salvation"*, definitively confirmed that Paul believed that God's promise of a new covenant was being fulfilled in that day (in that time period or generation).

"For He says: "In an acceptable time I have heard you, and in the day of salvation I have helped you." Behold, now is the accepted time; behold, now is the day of salvation." (2 Corinthians 6:2).

This new covenant could not however, be fully consummated until the Old Covenant had been fulfilled and had ultimately passed away. The writer to the Hebrews made it quite clear that although the Old Covenant had been made obsolete through the work of Christ, it was still in some sense in effect. It was growing old and ready to vanish away. Notice that the writer quotes directly from Jeremiah 31 as we did above. I believe that this vanishing away was finally completed as the temple and all that it represented were destroyed by the Roman armies in 70AD.

"Now this is the main point of the things we are saying: We have such a High Priest, who is seated at the right hand of the throne of the Majesty in the heavens, [2] a Minister of the sanctuary and of the true tabernacle which the Lord erected, and not man. [3] For every high priest is appointed to offer both gifts and sacrifices. Therefore it is necessary that this One also have something to offer. [4] For if He were on earth, He would not be a priest, since there are priests who offer the gifts according to the law; [5] who serve the copy and shadow of the heavenly things, as Moses was divinely instructed when he was about to make the tabernacle. For He said, "See that you make all things according to the pattern shown you on the mountain." [6] But now He has obtained a more excellent ministry, inasmuch as He is also Mediator of a better covenant, which was established on better promises. [7] For if that first covenant had been faultless, then no place would have been sought for a second. [8] Because finding fault with them, He says: "Behold, the days are coming, says the Lord, when I will make a new covenant with the house of Israel and with the house of Judah- [9] not according to the covenant that I made with their fathers in the day when I took them by the hand to lead them out of the land of Egypt; because they did not continue in My covenant, and I disregarded them, says the Lord. [10] For this is the covenant that I will make with the house of Israel after those days, says the Lord: I will put My laws in their mind and write them on their hearts; and I will be their God, and they shall be My people. [11] None of them shall teach his neighbor, and none his brother, saying, 'Know the Lord,' for all shall know Me, from the least of them to the greatest of them. [12] For I will be merciful to their unrighteousness, and their sins and their lawless deeds I will remember no more." [13] In that He says, "A new covenant," He has made the first obsolete. Now what is becoming obsolete and growing old is ready to vanish away" (Hebrews 8).

Paul said in Galatians 3:24 that the Old Covenant (Mosaic) law was a tutor to bring Israel to her Messiah. That was the ultimate purpose of the Old Covenant which by bringing them to Christ would no longer be needed. In fact it would be a hindrance to the complete restoration of relationship between God and His people (Israel, Judah and Gentiles according to Isaiah 49). Hebrews 9:8 said that "the way into the Holiest of All was not yet made manifest while the first tabernacle was still standing." The context of this passage clearly pertains to the earthly tabernacle or temple. Many commentators believe that it is not so much whether the physical temple is still physically standing, but whether it had standing as the way to access God. Its physical destruction would be a graphic demonstration that God no longer recognized this great symbol of the Old Covenant. Its destruction paved the way for full access to the greater and more perfect tabernacle not made with hands, where Christ had, with His own blood, entered the Most Holy Place. This is where His people would receive their eternal inheritance.

As the book of Hebrews asserts throughout, the new covenant was in every way far better than the first covenant. There was no longer any need for the blood of bulls and goats since Christ was the perfect sacrifice, having shed His own blood once for all. There was no need for the Levitical priesthood since Christ was the Mediator (the purpose of the priesthood) of the new covenant and was the High Priest of good things to come (Hebrews 9:11-15). There was no need for a physical temple since the Lord God Almighty and the Lamb are

135

their temple (Revelation 21:22) – that is those in Hebrews 12:22 who were said to have already come to Mount Zion and to the city of the living God, the heavenly Jerusalem.

All this essentially brings us back to where we began. In Leviticus 26:21, God said to Israel: "Then, if you walk contrary to Me, and are not willing to obey Me, I will bring on you seven times more plagues, according to your sins." We have already seen the importance of this whole passage (Leviticus 26), but now things really begin to come into focus if we jump forward from here to Revelation 15. We find this chapter beginning with a remarkable statement: "Then I saw another sign in heaven, great and marvelous: seven angels having the seven last plagues, for in them the wrath of God is complete" (Revelation 15:1). This fits perfectly with all that we have seen up to this point and would appear to tie directly to Leviticus 26:21 and the covenant judgment of Israel.

Even more compelling is the final verse of this short chapter: "The temple was filled with smoke from the glory of God and from His power, and no one was able to enter the temple till the seven plagues of the seven angels were completed" (Revelation 15:8). The temple has always represented or provided access to God and according to this verse no one could enter the temple until God's covenant wrath (expressed through the seven plagues) was complete. This was in a sense the climax of the covenant where the old fully passed away and the new was fully appropriated or consummated. This is one of the major reasons that more and more Christians are beginning to see how critically important the events of 70AD are in the history of the church.

Let me conclude by looking at a couple of related New Testament passages that I believe comport well with all that we have discussed

136

so far. As Jesus approached the end of His earthly ministry, He shared two parables that were directed specifically at the religious leaders of Jerusalem who, from what these texts clearly proclaim, recognized that Jesus was bringing accusations against them. His parables were likely a major stimulus for these leaders to intensify their efforts to finally bring Jesus' ministry to an end which they surely believed they had done through His crucifixion.

The later verses of Matthew 21 present what is commonly called The Parable of the Wicked Vinedressers, and as Jesus finished this brief tale it is very interesting to note the response of these men: "Now when the chief priests and Pharisees heard His parables, they perceived that He was speaking of them. But when they sought to lay hands on Him, they feared the multitudes, because they took Him for a prophet" (Matthew 21:45-46).

Jesus then followed with The Parable of the Wedding Feast which again was perceived by these men as an accusation and a threat made directly toward them as the religious leaders of Jerusalem. I will provide the entire text of this passage here because there are several key concepts present in this parable that may shed light on much of our previous discussion.

"And Jesus answered and spoke to them again by parables and said: ² "The kingdom of heaven is like a certain king who arranged a marriage for his son, ³ and sent out his servants to call those who were invited to the wedding; and they were not willing to come. ⁵ Again, he sent out other servants, saying, 'Tell those who are invited, "See, I have prepared my dinner; my oxen and fatted cattle are killed, and all things are ready. Come to the wedding."' But they made light of it and went their ways, one to his own farm, another to his business. ⁶ And

137

the rest seized his servants, treated them spitefully, and killed them. [7] But when the king heard about it, he was furious. And he sent out his armies, destroyed those murderers, and burned up their city. [8] Then he said to his servants, 'The wedding is ready, but those who were invited were not worthy. [9] Therefore go into the highways, and as many as you find, invite to the wedding.' [10] So those servants went out into the highways and gathered together all whom they found, both bad and good. And the wedding hall was filled with guests. [11] "But when the king came in to see the guests, he saw a man there who did not have on a wedding garment. [12] So he said to him, 'Friend, how did you come in here without a wedding garment?' And he was speechless. [13] Then the king said to the servants, 'Bind him hand and foot, take him away, and cast him into outer darkness; there will be weeping and gnashing of teeth.' [14] "For many are called, but few are chosen." [15] Then the Pharisees went and plotted how they might entangle Him in His talk." (Matthew 22:1-15).

There are a number of Old Testament passages that liken God's covenant with Israel to a marriage relationship (Isaiah 54:1-8; Jeremiah 3:1-10, 20; Jeremiah 31:31-32; Ezekiel 16 & 23; Hosea 1 & 2; Joel 1:1-10). Most of these passages focus on the unfaithfulness (or harlotry) of Israel as God's wife, and yet there are others that point to a time in Israel's future when God would remarry those whom He had previously divorced. This is seen in this beautiful passage from Hosea 2:

"And it shall be, in that day," says the LORD, "that you will call Me 'My Husband,' and no longer call Me 'My Master,' . . . "I will betroth you to Me forever; yes, I will betroth you to

138

Me in righteousness and justice, in lovingkindness and mercy;
I will betroth you to Me in faithfulness, and you shall know
the Lord" (Hosea 2:16, 19-20).

As we read through the New Testament and see Paul using language
related to this marriage theme in his instruction to the various
churches and as we see Jesus make use of wedding imagery, our
attention should be turned back to God's Old Testament promises to
remarry Israel by means of the establishment, through the blood of
the Lamb, of the promised new covenant.

The parable of the wedding feast pointed directly to the coming
wedding of the king's son. It spoke of the rejection of the invitations
sent out by the king's servants and ultimately deals with the fate of
those who reject this invitation to "come to the wedding." Verse 15
indicates that the Pharisees took this parable very personally, just as
had been the case upon hearing the parable of the wicked
vinedressers. These two parables both deal with the history of Israel
and their repeated refusal to heed the words of the prophets sent to
them by God, but also included the complicity of Jesus' 1st century
generation as they rejected those that He sent them.

Little if any time transpired in the transition from the end of Matthew
22 to the scathing words of Jesus found in Matthew 23. He continued
to direct His venomous charges and accusations toward the religious
leaders of His Jewish contemporaries. Beginning at verse 29, Jesus
again pointed to how it had been Israel who had killed the prophets
and that this present (1st century) generation would fill up the
measure of their father's sin by their treatment of the ones that Jesus
would send to them. Then He said that all the righteous blood shed on
the earth would be on them and that judgment would come upon this
(1st century) generation.

"Woe to you, scribes and Pharisees, hypocrites! Because you build the tombs of the prophets and adorn the monuments of the righteous, and say, 'If we had lived in the days of our fathers, we would not have been partakers with them in the blood of the prophets.' "Therefore you are witnesses against yourselves that you are sons of those who murdered the prophets. Fill up, then, the measure of your fathers' guilt. Serpents, brood of vipers! How can you escape the condemnation of hell? Therefore, indeed, I send you prophets, wise men, and scribes: some of them you will kill and crucify, and some of them you will scourge in your synagogues and persecute from city to city, that on you may come all the righteous blood shed on the earth, from the blood of righteous Abel to the blood of Zechariah, son of Berechiah, whom you murdered between the temple and the altar. Assuredly, I say to you, all these things will come upon this generation" (Matthew 23:29-36).

If we look closely at Revelation and in particular chapters 18 and 19, it will be seen that there are several verses from this section that must be understood as directly related to key concepts that we noted and discussed in Matthew 21-23. As seen above, the two parables both address Israel's ill treatment of the prophets (servants) sent to her. Jesus plainly stated in these two parables that it was previous generations of Israelites who had murdered the prophets and that it would be His own generation of Jews who would do the same to those sent by Jesus, and in doing so would fill up the measure of their father's guilt (Matthew 23:32).

140

Here in this section of Revelation is the following definitive statement in reference to Babylon: "And in her was found the blood of prophets and saints, and of all who were slain on the earth" (Revelation 18:24). Later in the 2nd verse of Chapter 19, is found another very critical declaration: "For true and righteous are His judgments, because He has judged the great harlot who corrupted the earth with her fornication; and *He has avenged on her the blood of His servants shed by her"* (Revelation 19:2, my emphasis).

Both these statements should be considered in relation to another important pronouncement made by Jesus in Luke's gospel: "Nevertheless I must journey, today, tomorrow, and the day following; for it cannot be that a prophet should perish outside of Jerusalem" (Luke 13:33). Note the complete agreement between Revelation 19:2 which explicitly stated that it was Babylon that had shed the blood of His servants (prophets), and Luke 13:33 where Jesus said that a prophet could not perish outside of Jerusalem. It seems to me quite clear from these two passages that Babylon of Revelation and Old Covenant Jerusalem are one and the same.

The identity of Babylon of Revelation is a subject of much controversy (I have written a book that deals with some of the most important issues that are critical for a proper identification of the great harlot), but here are two statements in the book of Revelation that also point directly to the statements made by Jesus that we have already examined in Matthew 21-23, and which must have a significant bearing on our understanding of this section of Revelation.

Note the first phrase from Revelation 19:2 – "For true and righteous are His judgments." This points back specifically to the original question that precipitated this whole discussion. When we see

141

references to God's judgments it is almost certain that this should point us back to Leviticus 26 and Deuteronomy 28 as well as the many subsequent Old Testament prophecies and warnings built upon those two crucial passages. I think we must always keep the prophet's warnings and promises of coming judgment within the context of God's covenant relationship with Israel. He sent His prophets to remind them that covenant judgment would surely come if they did not change their ways. True and righteous are His judgments precisely because they are the just response to Israel's disobedience, and these judgments are based on the provisions found in the stipulations of the covenant that God had made with her.

In this passage, heaven exalts over God's judgment of the great harlot and the cry goes forth that, "the Lord God Omnipotent reigns!" (Revelation 19:6). Then in the very next verse we are told that "the marriage of the Lamb has come" (Revelation 19:7). Two verses later John is told to write: "Blessed are those who are called to the marriage supper of the Lamb!" (Revelation 19:9). There are so many things here that precisely parallel Jesus' parable of the Wedding Feast. Note especially that the ones who had killed the servants were destroyed and the city was burned, and then came the wedding. Just so in Revelation 19, God *avenged on her* (Babylon) *the blood of His servants shed by her"* (Revelation 19:2), and then came the marriage of the Lamb (the Son).

Although it may seem quite strange to some, I think that all of this fits quite well with what happened in 70AD and that Babylon of Revelation was in fact representative of Old Covenant Jerusalem who had rejected her Messiah (recall John 19:15 where the chief priests replied to Pilot: "We have no king but Caesar!") and persecuted those sent to her by Jesus Christ. This would have also been the time when the seven last plagues, in which the covenant wrath of God was

142

completed (Revelation 15:1), took place. That means that the promised judgment (or plagues) found in Leviticus 26 and Deuteronomy 28, were fulfilled in the 70AD destruction of Jerusalem. True and righteous was God's response to the covenant unfaithfulness of those who had rejected His servants and ultimately rejected His Son. That is not the end of the story however. Since the seven last plagues (in which the vengeance of the covenant was poured out) have been completed, the people of God now have access to their God through the New Covenant that was established once for all through the shed blood of our Lord Jesus Christ.

"Then a mighty angel took up a stone like a great millstone and threw it into the sea, saying, "Thus with violence the great city Babylon shall be thrown down, and shall not be found anymore. The sound of harpists, musicians, flutists, and trumpeters shall not be heard in you anymore. No craftsman of any craft shall be found in you anymore, and the sound of a millstone shall not be heard in you anymore. The light of a lamp shall not shine in you anymore, and the voice of bridegroom and bride shall not be heard in you anymore. For your merchants were the great men of the earth, for by your sorcery all the nations were deceived. And in her was found the blood of prophets and saints, and of all who were slain on the earth." (19:1f) - After these things I heard a loud voice of a great multitude in heaven, saying, "Alleluia! Salvation and glory and honor and power belong to the Lord our God! For true and righteous are His judgments, because He has judged the great harlot who corrupted the earth with her fornication; and He has avenged on her the blood of His servants shed by her." Again they said, "Alleluia! Her smoke rises up forever and ever!" And the twenty-four elders and the four living creatures fell down and worshiped God who sat on the throne,

143

saying, "Amen! Alleluia!" Then a voice came from the throne, saying, "Praise our God, all you His servants and those who fear Him, both small and great!" And I heard, as it were, the voice of a great multitude, as the sound of many waters and as the sound of mighty thunderings, saying, "Alleluia! For the Lord God Omnipotent reigns! Let us be glad and rejoice and give Him glory, for the marriage of the Lamb has come, and His wife has made herself ready." And to her it was granted to be arrayed in fine linen, clean and bright, for the fine linen is the righteous acts of the saints. Then he said to me, "Write: 'Blessed are those who are called to the marriage supper of the Lamb!'" And he said to me, "These are the true sayings of God" (Revelation 18:21 - 19:9).

Although I struggled with them for some time, I've now come to the point where I don't see how the many time statements found throughout the New Testament and in particular the ones in Revelation that point to a fulfillment within the timeframe of that 1st century generation can be so easily ignored or explained away as many seem to do today. The last two passages that I present here for your consideration are Revelation 1:1-3 and Revelation 22:6 & 10, verses that essentially bracket the entire prophecy with identical claims that would seem to encompass the entire book. There are a number of other very explicit statements within this book which if taken in context seem to demand a 1st century fulfillment of Revelation. You may have come to a point where you can look at these statements and feel that it is acceptable, or perhaps even necessary to allow a 2000 year or more gap between the giving of these prophecies and their fulfillment, but I cannot read plain, straightforward statements that told 1st century readers of things that must shortly take place and not accept the fact that they did in fact take place in that generation.

"The Revelation of Jesus Christ, which God gave Him *to show His servants—things which must shortly take place.* And He sent and signified it by His angel to His servant John, [2] who bore witness to the word of God, and to the testimony of Jesus Christ, to all things that he saw. [3] Blessed is he who reads and those who hear the words of this prophecy, and keep those things which are written in it; *for the time is near"* (Revelation 1:1-3, my emphasis).

"Then he said to me, "These words are faithful and true." And the Lord God of the holy prophets sent His angel to show His servants the things which must shortly take place... And he said to me, "Do not seal the words of the prophecy of this book, for the time is at hand" (Revelation 22:6, 10).

The one major concept or premise that I believe is of great overriding importance for almost all aspects of biblical study and interpretation is that the Bible as we have it today is a document united in purpose in describing God's covenant relationship with the world that He created. Most of the Old Testament describes His covenantal dealings with a specific people, namely Israel and her forefathers, but with the ultimate goal that springing forth from them would come a seed, a servant, who through a promised new covenant with Israel and Judah would bless all the families of the earth. Almost every aspect of our study of this wonderful "book" must be conditioned by this overriding covenantal context.

I hope that these ramblings of mine will give you some things to seriously ponder. Over the past several years, I have tried in our class to lay a foundation for understanding some of these things. I've tried

145

to do this without pushing too hard or making as many direct or overt statements as I may have liked, because I know that this perspective seems very radical to many. Radical not because it deviates from the scriptures, but because it is so very different from what most of us have been taught and have believed for so many years.

Special Addendum by Don K. Preston

One Greater Than the Temple Is Here

To the early Jewish mind, nothing compared to the glory - and significance - of the Jerusalem Temple. As Wright has noted: "All the other symbols of ancient Israel and the second Temple Jewish world gathered around this majestic, potent building, and from it they took their meaning and power".[4] In an earlier work, Wright offered this: "The symbolism of the Temple was designed to express the belief that it formed the centre, not only of the physical world, but also of the entire cosmos, so that, in being YHVH's dwelling place, it was the spot where heaven and earth met."[5]

That temple represented several things. Wright lists a few:

1.) It symbolized the cosmos / world. The temple was actually referred to as "heaven and earth" and the very clothing of the High Priest likewise symbolized the cosmos. See Wright, (2013,101) where he cites the Wisdom of Solomon which "describes the robe of Aaron, the first high priest, as depicting 'the whole world' (*holos ho kosmos*)."

---

[4] N. T. Wright, *Paul and the Faithfulness* of God, (Minneapolis; Fortress, 2013), 101.

[5] N. T. Wright, Jesus *and the Victory of God*, Minneapolis; Fortress, 1996), 205.

2.) The Temple represented the David Kingdom. "Threats to the temple were threats to the king"- Thus, kingdom and temple are inextricably bound: "It is highly significant for our understanding of Paul, and his re-use of the Temple motif at various key points, that Temple and (Davidic) Messiahship go hand in hand." (P. 104).

3.) The destruction of the Temple therefore, led to a dissolution of the original world view and demanded a new one- thus, the predictions of the New Temple / Cosmos.

Stevenson adds that the Temple was the very symbol of Israel's election: "destruction of the temple could be seen as tantamount to the destruction of the nation." He calls attention to the fact that in Jewish thinking the Temple and Israel's place as the elect of God are tied together.[6]

Briggs concurs: "Both the power of Israel's God and the certainty of Israel's election were called into question. The divine covenant appeared to be sundered. Atonement could not be won upon the broken altars. Israel's millennial faith was shaken to its roots."[7]

---

[6] Gregory Stevenson, *Power and Place*, (New York; Walter De Gruyter, 2001), 128, see also 168.

[7] Robert Briggs, *Jewish Temple Imagery*, (New York; Peter Lang Publishing, 1999), 1; Briggs cites Kirschener, *Apocalyptic and Rabbinic Responses to the Destruction of A.D. 70*, HTR, 78 (1987)27-28 to the same effect.

Gentry calls attention to the covenantal significance of the Temple: "In essence the temple itself is a symbol: it symbolizes the *covenantal relationship* of God with His people. The heart of the covenant appears in the most important promise: 'I will be your God, you will be my people.' The temple is the special place where God dwells among His people."[8]

These citations, and many more could be given, demonstrate to a small degree how important the Temple was to the ancient Jews. (It should go without saying that we today have a difficult time grasping this mind-set, but, to properly understand the Bible, it behooves us to do so!) The temple represented the very presence of YHVH. It is where the God of the universe had placed His name!

With these historical facts in mind, let me say that in his personal ministry Jesus made some stunning statements. Those statements have been, even to modern times, almost overlooked in discussions about the deity of Christ and his "self-identity." In his debates with the Pharisees of his day, and in his actions in the temple, Jesus presented some ideas that when considered properly, force us to examine our concepts of Christology. Stay tuned!

We have taken note of the Jewish mind-set in regard to the Jerusalem Temple. It is so sad that many in modern day Christianity simply do not grasp how important that Temple was, not only in the mind of the Jews, but, in the eyes of God as well! We sometimes read comments like this, from Wayne Jackson:

---

[8] Kenneth Gentry, *He Shall Have Dominion*, (Draper, VA.; Apologetics Group, 2009), 362.

"What would the destruction of Jerusalem have meant to those people who were living in Athens, Greece? Paul says, 'Gentlemen, you had better repent.' Why? 'Because Jerusalem, hundreds of miles away is going to be destroyed in AD 70.' They likely would have said, 'So what!' What does that have to do with us?"[9]

Such a comment and question reveals either total desperation, total ignorance of the Jewish mind-set, or, a willingness to ignore the historical reality. In either case, Jackson's comments and question have no scholarly merit to them.

I should note that in formal debate, my Amillennial opponents have repeated this kind of "argument." In my formal debate with John Welch, (Indianapolis, 2008; MP3s of that debate are available from me) Welch put up a chart showing that Jerusalem was hundreds of miles away from Jerusalem, and asked, "Why would the Gentiles, hundreds of miles from Jerusalem care about the destruction of that Jewish city?" When I responded by asking why those same Gentiles should care about the death of a Jewish "rabble rousing, would be Messiah" on Golgotha, a shock went through the audience. The point being that if Gentiles should not be concerned with the fall of Jerusalem because it was so far away, then they should have no interest or concern about the death of Jesus. The fact is that in

---

[9]   Wayne Jackson, *The AD 70 Theory*, (Stockton, Ca., Courier Publications, 1990), 67, 79. I must say, as kindly as possible, that Jackson's book is one of the most illogical, poor attempts to respond to Covenant Eschatology that one will ever find.

151

prophecy, it was the end of the Old Covenant world that would fully open the way for salvation being offered to all men!

As we work our way to a consideration of the topic of our title, I think it good to examine the impact of the fall of Jerusalem on the ancient Jews. Now, keep in mind that as the title above suggests, I will be examining Jesus' statement in Matthew 12 that "one greater than the Temple is here." This stunning statement must be seen with the backdrop of understanding the Jewish concept of the importance of that physical edifice, and therefore, what the impact of its destruction would be on that mind-set. But more, the question is, when we examine the Jewish concepts of the Temple, and the reaction to its destruction, when we look then at Jesus' incredible claim, it raises the question of Christology in a powerful way! So, having seen how central to the Jewish mind the Temple was, what was - or what would be - the impact of the destruction of that Temple?

Consider first of all Matthew 24:2-3. Jesus predicted the utter desolation of that marvelous Temple. In direct response the disciples ask "When shall these things be, and what shall be the sign of your coming and the end of the age?"

As virtually all commentators agree, the disciples mentally connected the desolation of that Temple with the coming of Christ and the end of the age. Now, lamentably, most commentators believe the disciples were confused, or simply mistaken to make that connection, but the fact is that it was not Jesus' disciples who were confused, but modern commentators who fail or refuse to see that connection.

Consider now what scholarship has come to realize about the importance of the destruction of Jerusalem.

Stevenson shares this insight,

"Reacting to the destruction of Jerusalem in 70 C. E., Rabbi Simeon states: 'Since the day that the Temple was destroyed there has been no day without its curse; and the dew has not fallen in blessing and the fruits have lost their savour.' (Sot. 9:12)."[10]

N. T. Wright calls the events surrounding 66-70 "earth shaking."[11]

Meyers shares this information:

"The destruction of the Temple necessarily had cataclysmic political and religious consequences. Because the Temple had functioned as a political as well as cultic center, its loss left a vacuum into which the rabbis would move."[12]

"The destruction of the Second Temple in 70 C.E. constitutes, in most analyses, a watershed event for the Jews of antiquity. The elimination of the center, source of spiritual nourishment and preeminent symbol of the nation's identity, compelled Jews to reinvent themselves, to find other means of religious

---

[10] Gregory Stevenson, *Power and Place*, (New York; Walter De Gruyter, 2001), 128.

[11] N. T. Wright, *Jesus and the Victory of God*, (Minneapolis; Fortress, 1996), 362.

[12] Eric M. Meyers, *Cultures of the Jews: A New History*, David Biale Editor, (New York; Schocken Books, 2002.

sustenance, and to adjust their lives to an indefinite period of displacement." (Meyers, 2002,117).

"The loss of the Jerusalem Temple also meant that the Jewish religion had to transform itself from a Temple-based, sacrificial cult to a culture rooted in domestic and local practices." (Meyers, 2002, 163, 167).

Robert Briggs says, "With the destruction of Temple the image of the universe was rendered defective."[13]

Evangelical scholars have also begun to recognize the theological / redemptive / historical importance of the fall of Jerusalem. R. C. Sproul says: "No matter what view of eschatology we embrace, we must take seriously the redemptive-historical importance of Jerusalem's destruction in A.D.70."[14]

Likewise, Amillennialist Burton Coffman wrote: "The fall of Jerusalem was the greatest single event of a thousand years, and religiously significant beyond anything else that ever occurred in human history."[15]

---

[13] Robert Briggs, citing Safari, (*The Temple, Compendia Rerum Iudaicarum ad Novum Testamentum*, Vol. 2, Fortress, (906), 19, n. 64.

[14] R. C. Sproul, *The Last Days According to Jesus,* (Grand Rapids; Baker Books, 2000), 26.

[15] Burton Coffman, *Commentary on 1, 2 Peter*, (Abilene, Tx.; Abilene Christian University Press, 1979), 246.

In light of this information, and we could multiply this kind of scholarly insight many times over, for someone to claim that the fall of Jerusalem was a localized event, of no lasting spiritual significance, is the epitome of lack of learning, or a willful rejection of the facts.

With this information in mind then, we will examine the ministry of Jesus and his claims about himself and the Temple. One of Jesus' most astounding - yet commonly overlooked - statements is found in Matthew 12. To fully grasp the power of his words, I will give a good bit of the context:

> "At that time Jesus went through the grainfields on the Sabbath. And His disciples were hungry, and began to pluck heads of grain and to eat. And when the Pharisees saw it, they said to Him, 'Look, Your disciples are doing what is not lawful to do on the Sabbath!' But He said to them, 'Have you not read what David did when he was hungry, he and those who were with him: how he entered the house of God and ate the show bread which was not lawful for him to eat, nor for those who were with him, but only for the priests? Or have you not read in the law that on the Sabbath the priests in the temple profane the Sabbath, and are blameless? Yet I say to you that in this place there is One greater than the temple. But if you had known what this means, 'I desire mercy and not sacrifice,' you would not have condemned the guiltless. For the Son of Man is Lord even of the Sabbath" (Matthew 12:1-8).

This truly amazing statement that one (something) greater than the Temple was present, is sometimes (incredibly often!) overlooked in the literature, even in discussions of Christology and Jesus' self-identity as Messiah and Son of God. Yet there are some scholars who have glimpsed the power of the text.

Kiwoong Son says, "The transference of temple symbolism to Jesus himself is that the new temple is better than the old. 'I tell you that one greater than the temple is here (Matthew 12:6)'"[16]

Hays correlates Jesus' statement that "one (or *something*" since the Greek is in the neuter gender, yet the force is the same, dkp) greater than the Temple is here" with Matthew 1:21 - *Immanuel* - God with us:

> "If Jesus is 'God with us' then his personal presence now takes the place of the Temple where the presence of God was formerly thought to dwell. Writing his gospel in the aftermath of the catastrophic destruction of the Temple in Jerusalem, Matthew affirms that Jesus' presence is 'greater than the Temple' and thereby offers powerful assurance for his followers as well as a provocative challenge to those who reject him."[17]

---

[16] Kiwoong Son, *Zion Symbolism in Hebrews*. (Waynesboro, GA.; Paternoster,2005), 72.

[17] Richard Hays, *Looking Backward*, (Waco; Baylor University Press, 2014), 45.

Although he does not comment further on the significance of Jesus' words and claim, Hagner does say: "Given the great importance of the cultus, this statement is utterly astonishing in its significance." (Donald Hagner, *Word Biblical Commentary, Matthew 1-13*, Vol. 33a, (Dallas, Word Publishing, 1993)330.

For Jesus to claim that he was "greater than the Temple" is nothing less than the claim to be God. Only God could ever be considered greater than the Temple, which was the "home" of God! So, to reiterate, Jesus' claim was nothing short of stunning! But, it was not the last time Jesus made statements that, when properly understood, reveal to us his true identity.

Look at Matthew 24:35: "Heaven and earth will pass, but, my words will never pass away." It is common for commentators to all but gloss over this, or to minimize the Christological import of Jesus' words. What is commonly missed is, I suggest, a two-fold claim.

First, if we realize that the "heaven and earth" that Jesus is referring to may well have been the Jerusalem temple, which in the vernacular of the day was called "heaven and earth," then Jesus' words take on the significance of a covenant contrast. The Old Covenant, symbolized by that glorious temple, was supposed to pass, and so the disciples understood that in their questions in v. 3. So if Jesus was, as I develop in my book *The Elements Shall Melt With Fervent Heat*, saying that the glorious Old Covenant temple was going to pass, but that *his word, his covenant* (and by extension, his temple!) would endure forever, this is another, subtle but powerful way of saying, "something greater than the temple is here!" (On the note of the temple, see Hebrews 8:1 where the body of Christ is set forth as "the true tabernacle" as opposed to the Jerusalem temple.) The word "true" in the context is not "true versus false," but rather the idea that

157

Christ's temple is the body, the reality to which the Old Covenant Temple typologically pointed. It is the shadow versus the reality, and thus the temple of Christ is superior to the Jerusalem temple! Stunning stuff!

The next thing that would have been communicated to those disciples upon hearing Jesus' words was incredible, but perfectly in line with Matthew's claim that Jesus was "God with us." As Hays says:

> "Precisely because Jesus is Emmanuel, in his subsequent discourse on the end of the age (Matthew 24) he can offer the further remarkable assurance that his words will outlast all creation: "Heaven and earth will pass away, but, my words will not pass away" (Matthew 24:35). If we ask ourselves who might legitimately say such a thing, once again there can only be one answer: we find ourselves face-to-face with the God of the Old Testament. Isaiah gives definitive expression to this theological truth:

> "The grass withers, the flower fades, when the breath of the Lord blows upon it; surely the people are grass. The grass withers, the flower fades; but the word of our God will stand forever" (Isaiah 40:7-8). Christian interpreters lulled by familiarity with Matthew's Gospel may not fully appreciate the immense scope of the christological assertions made at every turn by Matthew. But there can be little doubt that the word spoken by Jesus in Matthew 24:35 can be true only if it is really is "the word of our God," only if the speaker who says "my words will not pass away" is in fact the God of Israel, God with us.'" (2014, 47). (I differ with Hays in his

view that Jesus contemplated the passing of material creation, as I indicate just above).

In Matthew 16:27-28 Jesus said that he was going to come in judgment of "every man." He was going to come "in the glory of the Father." As I demonstrate in my book *Like Father Like Son, On Clouds of Glory*, this statement meant not only that Jesus was going to come *in the same manner* as the Father had come many times before, but that in doing so, he would possess and manifest the Father's glory. This is confirmed by the fact that Matthew 16:27 is a strong echo of two Old Covenant predictions of the Day of the Lord.

In Isaiah 40, we find the prediction of the coming of the Voice, who would prepare for the coming of the Lord, the coming of *YHVH*. The Lord would come in judgment to reward the people (v. 10f). So when Jesus said that it was he that was coming to fulfill Isaiah 40, this was tantamount to saying that he is YHVH! The fact that John prepared the way for Jesus profoundly identifies Jesus as the God of Israel!

Consider another text from Isaiah that drives this point home in an undeniable way, and that is Isaiah 43, and the way that Jesus himself applied it:

> "Fear not, for I am with you; I will bring your descendants from the east, and gather you from the west; I will say to the north, 'Give them up!' And to the south, 'Do not keep them back!' Bring My sons from afar, and My daughters from the ends of the earth - everyone who is called by My name, whom I have created for My glory; I have formed him, yes, I have made him." Bring out the blind people who have eyes, and the deaf who have ears. Let all the nations be gathered together, and let the people be assembled. Who among them

159

can declare this, and show us former things? Let them bring out their witnesses, that they may be justified; or let them hear and say, "It is truth." "You are My witnesses," says the Lord, "And My servant whom I have chosen, that you may know and believe Me, and understand that I am He. Before Me there was no God formed, nor shall there be after Me. I, even I, am the Lord, and besides Me there is no savior. I have declared and saved, I have proclaimed, and there was no foreign god among you; Therefore you are My witnesses," says the Lord, "that I am God. Indeed before the day was, I am He; and there is no one who can deliver out of My hand; I work, and who will reverse it?" (Isaiah 43:5-13)

This incredibly rich text contains too many tenets to fully explore, but we will simply list a few "bullet points" for emphasis:

1. The Lord promised to restore / re-gather Israel. This is echoed in Matthew 8:11f.

2. YHVH promised to create a New People. See verses, 18-21.

3. That new people would include "all the nations" (v. 9).

4. Of this new creation the Lord said, "you shall be my witnesses" (v. 10).

5. They would be witnesses to the fact that:

"Before Me there was no God formed, nor shall there be after Me. [11] I, even I, am the Lord, and besides Me there is no savior" ... you are My witnesses," says the Lord, "that I am God. [13]. Indeed before the day was, I am He; and there is no one who can deliver out of My hand; I work, and who will reverse it?" (v. 11, 13).

6. In later verses, as God anticipated the new work that He would perform, He called on Israel to forget her past, and focus on the new thing that He would do! This is nothing less than astounding! Israel had always pointed to and gloried in her past. In fact, it is not too much to say that her past was her identity, for it was in the Exodus and Sinai that Israel was redeemed and given Torah, the marriage covenant. Thus, for the Lord to say that the new thing that He would do was so great, so wonderful, so dramatic, that Israel was to forget her past, is, to repeat, nothing less than incredible.

But, what does this have to do with our subject, the identity of Jesus? Everything! To "catch the power" of this, take a look at Acts 1.

"The former account I made, O Theophilus, of all that Jesus began both to do and teach, until the day in which He was taken up, after He through the Holy Spirit had given commandments to the apostles whom He had chosen, to whom He also presented Himself alive after His suffering by many infallible proofs, being seen by them during forty days and speaking of the things pertaining to the kingdom of God. And being assembled together with them, He commanded them not to depart from Jerusalem, but to wait for the Promise of the Father, "which," He said, "you have heard from Me; for John truly baptized with water, but you shall be baptized with the Holy Spirit not many days from now." 6 Therefore, when they had come together, they asked Him, saying, "Lord, will You at this time restore the kingdom to Israel?" And He said to them, "It is not for you to know times or seasons which the Father has put in His own authority. But you shall receive

161

power when the Holy Spirit has come upon you; and you shall be witnesses to Me in Jerusalem, and in all Judea and Samaria, and to the end of the earth" (Acts 1:1-8).

Take note:

1. The risen Jesus, the Christ who was, "declared to be the Son of God through the Spirit of holiness, by the resurrection from the dead" (Romans 1:4) directs his apostles, who will become the representatives of the New Israel, to go tell the world of him.

2. As he prepares to ascend to the Father, he assembles those disciples, who would sit on twelve thrones, judging the tribes of Israel" (Matthew 19:28). When Mattathias is chosen to fill the number of the "twelve," we thus have the leaders, the judges, of the new creation in place, and on the day of Pentecost they began judging Israel through the proclamation of "life or death" based on the acceptance or rejection of the message of Jesus, the Messiah (cf. Acts 3:21f; 2 Corinthians 2:14f).

3. Notice that in Isaiah, we are told that YHVH is the One, True and exclusive Savior - there is none else. And what do we find when the disciples of Jesus, sent to bear witness of him, proclaim? We find them declaring: "Nor is there salvation in any other, for there is no other name under heaven given among men by which we must be saved." They declare that this Jesus is the One True and Only Savior!

4. Those apostles would "be my witnesses" in Jerusalem, Judea, Samaria and to the uttermost parts of the earth" (v. 8). Virtually all critical scholars agree that Jesus was citing Isaiah 43:10. (I suggest that Isaiah 43 serves as the template for the book of Acts). This being so, the application to our topic is direct and incredible.

162

In Isaiah, Israel was to bear witness of the One True God - YHVH. The Lord said, "You are MY witnesses." Israel was to be the light to the nations, proclaiming His name. But now, in Acts 1, Jesus the Risen Messiah tells his disciples – citing Isaiah 43 - "You are MY witnesses!"

Jesus is clearly, undeniably, associating himself as the Lord of heaven and earth! He is saying he is the One True God. He is the only Savior! Now clearly, he is not calling himself the Father since the Father sent him, but he is nonetheless saying, just as we will see that John 5:21f attests, that men are to now know him and to worship him, just as they worship the Father!

Acts 1 therefore, becomes an incredible "witness," pun intended, to the identity of Jesus. He is not a mere man. And this has a direct bearing on our understanding of the purpose, not only of the world mission, but, the purpose of Christ's promised coming in judgment. Jesus' coming in judgment was to reveal him as "King of kings and Lord of lords," not as a man in the body of his humiliation. It would be by his coming in judgment that he would be seen for who he truly is, "You are MY witnesses"– he is God!

Temple has shown us above the repeated statements in the Old Covenant scriptures where virtually every time the Lord was to come in judgment, He said He was going to do that, "So that they may know that I am God." And to miss this identical purpose in the coming of Christ is to miss the very reason for his coming. He was not merely coming to judge. He was coming to judge so that all men might honor the Son as they honor the Father." More on that momentarily.

In a similar vein, Matthew 16:27 is a strong echo of Isaiah 62, and the prediction of the "remarriage" of Israel to the Lord. YHVH had divorced the ten northern tribes (Hosea 2:1-3), but promised that in the last days He would come and marry her (Hosea 2:18f). Isaiah 62 picks up that prediction and promised that in the great Day of the Lord's coming:

> "Indeed the Lord has proclaimed to the end of the world: "Say to the daughter of Zion, 'Surely your salvation is coming; Behold, His reward is with Him, And His work before Him.'" And they shall call them The Holy People, the Redeemed of the Lord; and you shall be called Sought Out, a City Not Forsaken."

So in Isaiah 40 and 62 the coming of YHVH was promised. But in both Matthew 3 and Matthew 16:27, John said it was Jesus who was about to come in judgment, fulfilling those prophecies and, Jesus himself said that those prophecies foretold *his* parousia in judgment! Thus Jesus' statement that he was to come "in the glory of the Father" is incredibly important for our understanding of who Christ claimed to be - and is. Wright expresses it like this:

> "The long awaited return of YHWH is, I suggest, the hidden clue to the origin of Christology."

Wright points out that in the OT, it was YHWH that promised to return. It was YHWH that was going to dwell with Israel / mankind. It was YHVH who would "visit" His people. In the NT, Jesus is posited as fulfilling those promises!

164

"Israel's God had done what He had long promised. He had returned as king. He had "visited" his people and "redeemed" them. Jesus had done what God said he and he alone would do. Early Christology did not begin, I suggest, as a strange new belief based on memories of earlier Jewish language for mediator-figures, or even on the strong sense of Jesus' personal presence during worship and prayer, important though that was as well. ...The most important thing was that in his life, death and resurrection, Jesus had accomplished the new Exodus, had done in person what Israel's God had said he would do in person. He had inaugurated God's kingdom on earth as in heaven. ....What matters most is the pre-Christian Jewish ideas about Israel's God. *Jesus' first followers found themselves not only (as it were) permitted to use God-language for Jesus, but compelled to use Jesus-language for the One God.*"[18]

Long adds this:

"If Jesus is described in terms of the bridegroom hosting a wedding banquet at the end of the age, then imagery from the Hebrew Bible which originally described God is re-applied to Jesus. But this is not unusual. There are a number of examples of Jesus applying language which originally applied to God to himself."[19]

---

[18] N. T. Wright, *Paul and the Righteousness of God*, Vol. I & II, (Minneapolis; Fortress, 2013), 654.

[19] Philipp Long, *Jesus the Bridegroom*, (Eugene, Or; Pickwick Publications, 2013), 146.

It is a tremendous theological tragedy to overlook or to mitigate these statements by Jesus as to his "self-identity." Another text confirms this.

Notice John 5:22-23:

> "For the Father judges no one, but has committed all judgment to the Son, that all should honor the Son just as they honor the Father. He who does not honor the Son does not honor the Father who sent Him."

The Father had committed all judgment to the Son. The Son would act in judgment as he had seen the Father judge. And the reason for this was, "*that* (Greek '*hina*' meaning, 'in order that') all men might honor the Son as (in the same manner) that they honor the Father." Something very important is stated here.

Now, if the Father committed the judgment authority and prerogative to the Son so that men might honor the Son *in the same way that they honor Him*, this speaks powerfully and eloquently of the nature of Jesus. He truly is "Immanuel" – "God with us!" By manifesting his judgment authority, Jesus was to be manifested, not as man, but as God! There is a dominant Old Testament concept found here.

In the Tanakh, one of the most common statements to be found, in direct connection to the judgments of God, was, "that they may know that I am God!" In the book of Ezekiel, for instance, this phrase is used some 82 times, if my count is correct. In other words, YHVH sent His prophets to inform people that He was about to act, most often in acts of judgment on a given nation. In warning that object

166

nation or people of what was about to come, the Lord said that when they would see those things come to pass, they would know that YHVH was the One, True, Sovereign God.

So God, acting in judgment, manifested Himself so that people would honor Him and know who He is. In a highly evocative text, Isaiah said that in those acts of judgment, the righteous would know that it was YHVH at work. They would know that it was the Day of the Lord that had come. The wicked on the other hand, would see the same actions take place, and either not recognize that it was YHVH at work, or they would refuse to acknowledge it, until it was too late (Isaiah 26:9f).

To say that this has incredible implications in John 5, not to mention a host of other texts, is a huge understatement! Just as the Father had acted in judgment to demonstrate His sovereignty and reveal His "identity," He had now committed that same judgment prerogative and authority to the Son, who would act in judgment as the Father had acted, "So that all men might honor the Son as they honor the Father."

Several NT texts that speak of the coming of Christ in judgment point us in this same direction.

Matthew 24:30, speaking of Christ's coming in judgment of Old Covenant Jerusalem, says that in those events the witnesses would see, "the sign of the Son of Man in the heavens." Commentators have noted that Jesus was not saying the inhabitants of Jerusalem would see something in the sky. No, the idea is that in seeing the fulfillment of Jesus' prophecy, those fulfilling events would point to the fact that Jesus was, "King of kings and Lord of lords"! Just as the Father judged "so that you may know that I am God", Jesus would act likewise, so that men would know who He is! Take note of just a few comments.

Gibbs shows that, "the sign of the Son of Man in heaven" is not a visible sign in the sky, but that the fall of Jerusalem was the sign of Christ's enthronement in the heavens.20

DeMar says, "Jesus was not telling his disciples that He would appear in the sky. ....Jesus told his disciples that they would see a sign that proved He was in the heaven, sitting at His Father's right hand."[21]

Gentry agrees:

> "The final collapse of Jerusalem will be the sign that the Son of Man, whom the Jews reject and crucify, is in heaven (Matthew 24:30). The fulfillment of his judgment-word demonstrates his heavenly position and power (cf. Dt. 18:22). ...Through these events the Jews would "see" the Son of Man in his judgment-coming in terrifying cloud-glory: clouds symbolize his divine majesty by stormy destruction (Is. 19:16-21; Is. 61:1-3; cf. Lev. 25:9-10)."[22]

---

20 Jeffrey A. Gibbs, *Jerusalem and Parousia*, St. Louis, MO; Concordia Academic Press, 2000), 198f.

[21] Gary DeMar, *Last Days Madness*, (Powder Springs, Ga; American Vision, 1999), 165.

[22] Kenneth Gentry, *He Shall Have Dominion*, (Draper, VA.; Apologetics Group, 2009), 355.

168

Mathison concurs:

> "The Greek text of this verse does not state that the Son of Man will appear in the heavens. Rather, what appears is the *sign* of the Son of Man in heaven. In other words, the destruction of Jerusalem will be the sign that the Son of Man, who prophesied this destruction, is in heaven." [23]

Perriman also points us in that same direction when commenting on Matthew 24:26. He comments on the reference to the parousia being as the lightning, and how some insist that this demands a literal, bodily appearance of Jesus, as a man that could be found in the desert: i.e. "he is in the desert or in the inner room."

Perriman rejects that idea:

> "This powerful image (lightning, DKP) has usually been understood to describe the effulgence of Christ's bodily coming at the end of the age. The contrast, however, is not with the ordinariness of these imposters - after all, they will perform great "signs and wonders" - but with the false announcements about a concrete, localized and embodied mode of being. A more careful reading of the simile suggests

---

[23] Keith Mathison, *Postmillennialism: An Eschatology of Hope*, (Philippsburg, NJ; P&R Publishing, 1999), 114.

169

that it signifies the immaterial and universal nature of Christ's *presence*."[24]

This agrees with the comments above about the "sign of the Son of Man." Jesus was not predicting that he was going to come as a 5' 5" Jewish man on the literal clouds. He was going to act in judgment as the Father had acted in judgment, and in and through those actions - fulfilling the prophecies - *he would be recognized as the Son of God* - the King of kings and Lord of lords! Origen recognized this early on.

Dunn cites Origen who noted that critics of Christianity who based their case on the interpretation of Scripture "failed to notice that the prophecies speak of two advents of Christ. In the first he is subject to human passions and deeper humiliation...in the second he is *coming in glory and in divinity alone*, without any human passions bound up with his divine nature."[25]

Consider this concept of Jesus' prediction in light of what the OT said about YHVH and the honor due to him:

Isaiah 48:11: "For My own sake, for My own sake, I will do it; for how should My name be profaned? And I will not give My glory to another." The Father said that only He is worthy of Glory. He said He would not give the glory to anyone else. Only "God" possesses that

---

[24] Andrew Perriman, *The Coming of the Son of Man*, (London; Paternoster, 2005), 35f.

[25] James D. G. Dunn, *Jews and Christians the Parting of the Ways*, (Grand Rapids; Eerdmans, 1992), 112. My emphasis).

170

divine identity and right to receive worship. *And yet* in the NT, Jesus emphatically said that before the world began, he *possessed that Glory with the Father* (John 17:5). He said he was going to act in judgment - the Divine prerogative of judgment - so that all men might honor him "as they honor the Father." *The Son is not the Father,* but he is "one" with the Father (John 10:30) and it is the Father's intent that *all men honor His Son as they honor Him*! And make no mistake, Jesus accepted that honor, he accepted *worship*.

Observe Jesus' temptation in light of Matthew's following account of how Jesus accepted worship (*proskuneo*). Satan wanted to be worshiped, but Jesus said only God is worthy of such. With that in mind, remember that Matthew posits Jesus as "God with us" (Immanuel). Then in the numerous pericopes of his ministry, *Jesus accepts worship!* (*proskuneo*). It must be noted - as Hayes does, (2014, 44) - that to *proskuneo* someone does not *always demand* the idea of "worship" i.e. the adulation of Deity. There are several examples of this in the Gospels. Nonetheless, there are examples in the Gospels in which the word and the context virtually demands that Jesus was accepting worship that was / is due only to *God*.

When Jesus walked on the waters and stilled the storm in Matthew 14, we are told that in response to this incredible demonstration, the disciples "Worshiped him, saying, 'Truly you are the Son of God'" (Matthew 14:33). Modern readers, not properly knowledgeable of Torah, commonly miss what I will call "the echo of Divinity" that is latent in this text.

Matthew was a Hebrew, writing to a Hebrew audience. Those readers would almost certainly have instantly recognized the incredible power and implications of this story. In the Tanakh, only YHVH walked on the sea! Only the Lord of Heaven calmed the storms! As

171

Hays says, "The worship of the disciples acknowledges and declares Jesus' identity with the one God of Israel, present in the midst of His people." (2014, 44). When one considers the Old Covenant identity of YHVH as the Lord of creation, and compares that with what happened in Matthew 14, it does not do justice to the story to say that the disciples were simply saying, "Sir, you are a really great guy!" They *worshiped* Jesus! Why? Were they simply saying that he was an impressive personage? No, "Truly, you are the Son of God!" Keep in mind that in this narrative Jesus accepts from his disciples what he had strictly refused to offer Satan, insisting that none but God is worthy of that, and in the words of the disciples it is indisputably clear that they are ascribing to Jesus the right to receive that *proskuneo* - worship!

As suggested above, when we examine the purpose of Jesus' parousia as stated in several passages, it becomes more than apparent that the purpose of the "Second Coming" as it is generally called, was not - to reiterate my point - to reveal Jesus as a 5' 5" Jewish man! This is a tremendously important reality because the widely held view of eschatology is that when the disciples were promised that Jesus was going to come "In like manner as you have seen him go" (Acts 1:9f), that this demands the physical appearing at the end of human history, when Jesus, a 5' 5" Jewish man comes out of heaven riding on a cumulus cloud. This completely misses the point of the purpose of Christ's parousia.

Christ was not to return to reveal himself as a *man*. The Incarnation did that! But the Incarnation was Jesus in "the body of humiliation." It was the man Jesus, "made a little lower than the angels." It was Jesus, who "in the days of his flesh" (Hebrews 5:7- which strongly implies that the "days of flesh" were in the past when Hebrews was written!), had put off 'the form (*morphe*) of God' humbling himself

172

so much as to be in the fashion of a servant. (See Philippians 2-3). But Jesus was not going to be revealed in the body of flesh, in the form of a servant, at his parousia. Notice just a key text or two:

1 Timothy 6:14-15f - Paul encouraged Timothy to, "Keep this commandment without spot, blameless until our Lord Jesus Christ's appearing, which He will manifest in His own time, He who is the blessed and only Potentate, the King of kings and Lord of lords." Keep in mind that Matthew 16:27, Matthew 24:30f; John 5:21f, have already informed us that the purpose of the parousia was not to reveal the Father, but *to reveal the Son, as the Son of God*, for men to honor Him! The "epiphany" of Christ's coming would reveal his true identity: the King of kings and Lord of lords!

Titus 2:13-14 – "Looking for the blessed hope and glorious appearing of our great God and Savior Jesus Christ, who gave Himself for us, that He might redeem us from every lawless deed and purify for Himself His own special people, zealous for good works." They were looking for Jesus - the Christ. Their "blessed hope" was the glorious appearing of the great God, the Savior, Jesus Christ!

Revelation 19:10-16:

"Now I saw heaven opened, and behold, a white horse. And He who sat on him was called Faithful and True, and in righteousness He judges and makes war. His eyes were like a flame of fire, and on His head were many crowns. He had a name written that no one knew except Himself. He was clothed with a robe dipped in blood, and His name is called The Word of God. And the armies in heaven, clothed in fine linen, white and clean, followed Him on white horses. Now

173

out of His mouth goes a sharp sword, that with it He should strike the nations. And He Himself will rule them with a rod of iron. He Himself treads the winepress of the fierceness and wrath of Almighty God. And He has on His robe and on His thigh a name written:

"KING OF KINGS AND
LORD OF LORDS."

Notice that this "One" judges and makes war - this is Jesus acting with the Divine Judgment prerogative vested to him by the Father. Furthermore, when we compare this vision with Revelation 1:8 the point is magnified:

"I am the Alpha and the Omega, the Beginning and the End," says the Lord, "who is and who was and who is to come, the Almighty."

While some MSSs omit "Alpha and Omega" nonetheless in the text it seems Jesus is speaking of himself, identifying himself as "the first and the last" which takes us directly back to Isaiah 41:4, where YHVH said: "I, the Lord, am the first; and with the last I am He." Thus Jesus' self-identification in Revelation 1:8 is stunning, but when we conflate Revelation 1:8 and chapter 19, it comprises a powerful testimony about who Jesus is - the Lord of Glory.

This vision in Revelation 19 reminds us somewhat of the vision in Isaiah 6 (not to mention the Transfiguration), where the prophet saw the Lord - YHVH, sitting on the throne, exalted. But do not forget that in John 12:40-41, the apostle said that Isaiah saw YHVH seated on the throne!

174

The text says that this "One" would tread the winepress of the fierceness and wrath of Almighty God. In the OT, it is YHVH that trod the nations in the winepress of His fury:

"Why is Your apparel red, and Your garments like one who treads in the winepress? 'I have trodden the winepress alone, and from the peoples no one was with Me. For I have trodden them in My anger, and trampled them in My fury; their blood is sprinkled upon My garments, and I have stained all My robes." (Isaiah 63:2-3).

This is YHVH coming in judgment, "to make for yourself a glorious name" (Isaiah 63:14).

When the Lord brought the Babylonians against Jerusalem, Jeremiah the prophet looked back on that judgment and "lamented": "The Lord has trampled underfoot all my mighty men in my midst; He has called an assembly against me to crush my young men; the Lord trampled as in a winepress the virgin daughter of Judah" (Lamentations 1:15). Notice now that in Revelation 14, the one like the Son of Man is the one that treads out the winepress of God's wrath (Revelation 14:14f). The link, the identity, is undeniable.

What we see in these and a host of other OT texts is that it was the Father who had acted in judgment. He had "come" many times before. Yet it should be patently obvious that in none of those occasions did He appear as a man, riding on the clouds, literally descending out of heaven. And when YHVH came in all of those instances, it was to manifest Himself and His glory so that men would honor Him. With this in mind, I want to call attention to one of the foundational NT texts of the so-called "Second Coming" of Christ, that we are assured is yet to occur at the end of time. That text is 2 Peter 3.

For brevity, I will offer this. The expanded discussion can be found in my book, *The Elements Shall Melt With Fervent Heat.*

2 Peter 3 anticipated the fulfillment of Isaiah 63-66, the prophecy of the new heavens and earth that would be fully established at the Day of the Lord (2 Peter 3:1-2, v. 13).

The prophecy of Isaiah 63-66 anticipated the coming of the Lord out of heaven when the mountains would melt under His feet (Isaiah 64:1f), and His name would be made manifest to the nations. (This is another way of expressing "so that they may know that I am God").

The prophecy of Isaiah 63-66 actually goes back further than chapter 63. It includes the prophecy of Isaiah 62 and the promise that in the last days YHVH would once again marry Israel. This would be in the Day of His coming for salvation (62:4f). This prophecy serves as the source for Jesus' prediction of his parousia in Matthew 16:27, and of course, he said that would occur in his generation (Matthew 16:28).

The coming of the Lord foretold in Isaiah 63-66 to bring in the new creation, was to be the same as when the Lord had come before "when you came down, the mountains shook at your presence" (Isaiah 64:1-4). Isaiah looks back on previous events in which YHVH had come manifesting His sovereignty, revealing His Deity.

The previous Days of the Lord were non-literal, non-bodily descents of the Lord out of heaven. Literal heaven and earth never perished

176

before. YHVH came by means of historical events under His sovereign control. He made known His name!

Since the Day of the Lord of Isaiah 63-66 was to be of the same non-literal, non-bodily, non-visible coming as previous Days of the Lord, and since the Day of the Lord of 2 Peter 3 was to be the fulfillment of the prediction of Isaiah 63-66, it therefore follows that the Day of the Lord of 2 Peter 3 was to be a non-literal, non-bodily, non-visible Day of the Lord. With this background of 2 Peter, and then harmonizing the text with what we have seen in John 5:21f, this should be proof positive that 2 Peter 3 is not about a future coming of a 5' 5" Jewish man out of heaven to show that he is man in the flesh! *This is Jesus being revealed as God!*

So 2 Peter 3, when seen through the prism of Isaiah 64-66, serves as incredible proof that the Second Coming was never intended to be understood as the revelation (*apocalupsis*) of Jesus, once again, as a man in the flesh. It was to posit Him as exercising the Divine prerogative of judgment so that the nations might know that you are God!

You must catch the power of this indisputable fact in comparison and application of Revelation 19: This vision of Revelation 19 is not a vision of *the "man" Jesus in his Incarnate body of flesh.* The vision of Christ in Revelation in no way resembles Jesus' Incarnate body of flesh - does it?

Revelation 1:12f describes a post-Ascension appearance of Jesus, to John on Patmos:

177

"Then I turned to see the voice that spoke with me. And having turned I saw seven golden lampstands, [13] and in the midst of the seven lampstands One like the Son of Man, clothed with a garment down to the feet and girded about the chest with a golden band. His head and hair were white like wool, as white as snow, and His eyes like a flame of fire; His feet were like fine brass, as if refined in a furnace, and His voice as the sound of many waters; He had in His right hand seven stars, out of His mouth went a sharp two-edged sword, and His countenance was like the sun shining in its strength."

It would be completely misplaced to suggest that Jesus' appearance here is his "Incarnate body form." This appearance is more than a little similar to the Transfiguration scene:

"He was transfigured before them. His face shone like the sun, and His clothes became as white as the light. And behold, Moses and Elijah appeared to them, talking with Him. Then Peter answered and said to Jesus, 'Lord, it is good for us to be here; if you wish, let us make here three tabernacles: one for You, one for Moses, and one for Elijah.' While he was still speaking, behold, a bright cloud overshadowed them; and suddenly a voice came out of the cloud, saying, 'This is My beloved Son, in whom I am well pleased. Hear ye Him!'" (Matthew 17:2-6).

Now Peter makes it clear in 2 Peter 1:16f that the Transfiguration was a vision of the "Second Coming" of Christ, his parousia. This is fatal to the view that Jesus is to be revealed from heaven in his Incarnate body of flesh - to reveal him as a man once again.

Exactly how did the Transfigured Jesus resemble the Incarnate body of Jesus? If the Second Coming of Jesus is - as claimed - to reveal him in his Incarnate body of flesh - *then why was he transfigured*? Why was his "form" so radically, dramatically altered, so much so that it terrified his disciples who had never been frightened by his appearance beforehand? Where is there even a hint of likeness in his Incarnate body of flesh and that awe inspiring, fear inducing Transfiguration vision?

The reason is quite simple. Jesus' parousia was not to reveal him as a man. It was not for him to show up in his body of humiliation, the body of flesh, in the "form" of the servant- man. It was to reveal him as the Son of God, the True God, the King of kings and Lord of lords!

Just as the Transfiguration was not a vision of Jesus as man, but was a vision of the Second Coming, so the vision of Christ at his parousia in Revelation 19 is likewise not a vision of a 5' 5" Jewish man in the form of a servant. If Jesus' Incarnate, servant body of flesh is to be the body of his parousia, why does the vision in Revelation 1 and 19 not resemble that Incarnate body of flesh? Not even remotely so! This is not Jesus "in the days of his flesh." *This is Jesus, to be sure.* But this coming is clearly not to reveal him as Incarnate man. It is to reveal him as "King of kings and Lord of lords." It is to reveal him as the one greater than the Temple!

Let me address an objection here. It is often argued that if Jesus does not come back in his incarnate body of flesh that it is not truly Jesus. In other words, the argument is that Jesus in a different form - a form different from his incarnate, 5' 5" human body of flesh, then it is not truly Jesus. This form of argument was offered by my debate opponent Jason Wallace, in a formal debate held in Salt Lake City,

Utah in 2015. You can view that debate on YouTube here: https://www.youtube.com/watch?v=PjOMCLbPhvc).

Likewise, in numerous Internet exchanges I have had this same form of argument offered against preterism. But this argument fails on many, many levels. For brevity, I will give only a few bullet points for consideration.

1) Consider the logical corollary to the argument that Jesus in a different form is not Jesus.

Prior to his incarnation, Jesus was "in the form" (*morphe*) of God, but he divested himself of that "form" and became man (Philippians 2:5f). He took on the form of man. He was no longer in the "form of God." Thus if it is the case that Jesus in a different form is not Jesus, then John was patently wrong when he said, "The Word became flesh and dwelt among men" (John 1:14). The Word patently changed forms, but would anyone seriously argue that he was no longer the Word?

2) In Mark 16:9, 12 we are told that after his resurrection, Jesus appeared in a "different form" *(heteras morphe)* to the disciples. So we have the emphatic declaration that after his passion, after his resurrection, he appeared in a different form! So once again, if it is the case that Jesus in a different form is not Jesus, then after his resurrection, Jesus was not Jesus!

3) In the Transfiguration accounts, we are told that Jesus' form was radically altered (from *metamorphoo*, from whence we get *metamorphosis*). He no longer appeared in the form of his incarnate body. That is irrefutably true, for the disciples were frightened speechless by his radical transformation. Yet during their time with

him for 3 years, they had never been alarmed at his physical appearance. So once again, we have Jesus in *a different form*, yet no one would seriously deny that the transfigured Jesus was actually Jesus. The desperate nature of the "Jesus in a different form is not Jesus" argument should be more than obvious, and it was for the audience in the aforementioned debate. My opponent had no answer at all.

(For an expanded discussion of the Transfiguration as a vision of the Second Coming of Christ, see my *Like Father Like Son, On Clouds of Glory* book. As a vision of the "Second Coming" the Transfiguration completely falsifies all claims that Jesus' parousia was to be his "re-appearance" in the body of flesh, revealed once again as a mere man).

There is so much more that could be written here, but hopefully this will suffice to help the reader to see how important the words of Jesus in Matthew 12:6 truly are. While some commentators give passing note of how "utterly astounding" those words are, it is amazing how little critical attention the text is given. But when we take Jesus' words seriously, and especially in comparison with the texts that speak of his parousia, his self-identity as one "greater than the temple" negates any concept of a coming "in a body of flesh" to reveal him as a *man*. His incarnation was to reveal him as a man, as a servant, of "flesh and blood." In his parousia, however, as one greater than the Temple, Jesus was to be revealed as "King of kings and Lord of lords" - not in the form of one "a little lower than the angels!" He came in glory, as the Father had come in glory so many times before, "so that they may know that I am the Lord."

It is our hope that this book will help the reader to appreciate the purpose of Christ's coming. While many Bible students (rightly) see

Christ's coming for the purpose of bringing salvation, or to judge the wicked, it is unfortunate that his "Second Coming" is not seen for what it truly was intended (in addition to these other purposes). His coming was to reveal him as God.

For more on the questions of the Deity of Christ, see the excellent series of articles by Joe Daniels on Don K. Preston's website. The first of the articles can be found here:

http://eschatology.org/index.php?option=com_k2&view=item&id=1 496:is-jesus-truly-god&Itemid=61.

Suggested Reading:

There is an ever growing body of literature dealing with fulfilled prophecy. This includes many valuable books and pamphlets as well as numerous articles and books available online. Listed below are several websites that contain a wealth of information in addition to a list of suggested books that address a wide range of topics related to the vast scope of fulfilled eschatology, including material discussed in this document. All of the books listed below may be obtained either directly from or through Amazon.com. All of Don Preston's books as well as several others listed below are available through his websites www.eschatology.org and www.bibleprophecy.com. Many of these books are also available at Amazon.com. Don Preston also has a number of excellent teaching series available in audio and video formats. These can be purchased from his websites as well. In addition, you can find a great deal of teaching by Don Preston on YouTube.

Websites:

http://www.eschatology.org
http://www.bibleprophecy.com/
http://www.bereanbiblechurch.org/home.php
http://home.ad70.net/
http://www.fulfilledcg.com/Site/Magazine/magazine.htm
http://www.bibleprophecy.com/
http://www.asiteforthelord.com/id15.html
http://prophecydebate.com/
http://tfcmag.com/index.php

Books:

Bray, John L., *Matthew 24 Fulfilled*, (Powder Springs, GA, American Vision) 2008.

Chilton, David, *The Days of Vengeance*, (Tyler, Tx., Institute for Christian Economics) 2011.

Collins, Tina Rae, *The Gathering in the Last Days*, (New York, NY., M. F. Sohn Publications) 2012.

Dawson, Sam, *Essays on Eschatology*, (Amarillo, Tx. PDP Publishing) 2009.

Demar, Gary, *Last Days Madness*, (Powder Springs, GA, American Vision) 1999.

Denton, T. Everett, *Hebrews: From Flawed to Flawless*, (Available www.eschatology.org.) 2011.

Russell, J. Stuart, *The Parousia*, (Grand Rapids, MI., Baker Books) 1999.

Frost, Sam, *Exegetical Essays on the Resurrection*, (Ardmore, Ok., JaDon Publishing) 2010.

Gentry, Kenneth, *Before Jerusalem Fell*, (Fountain Inn, SC., Victorious Hope) 2010.

The Beast of Revelation, (Tyler, Tx., Institute for Christian Economics) 1989.

184

Green, David; Sullivan, Michael; Hassertt, Edward, *House Divided*, (Ramona, CA., Vision Publishing) 2009.

Gumerlock, Francis X., *Revelation and the First Century Preterist Interpretations of the Apocalypse in Early Christianity*, (Powder Springs, GA., American Vision) 2012.

Harden, Daniel E., *Gathered Into the Kingdom: Preterist Theology, Expectations, and 1 Thessalonians 4:17: An Examination of Eschatology with a View on the Preterist Model and Three Preterist Views of the Rapture Event*, (CreateSpace Independent Publishing Platform) 2013.

Hill, Glenn, *Christianity's Great Dilemma*, (Lexington, Ky., Moonbeam Publications) 2010.

King, Max. R., *The Cross and the Parousia of Christ*, (Warren, OH, Writing and Research Miinstry, Parkway Rd. Church of Christ) 1987.

The Spirit of Prophecy, (Warren, OH, Warren Printing) 1990.

Martin, Brian, *Behind the Veil of Moses*, (Xulon) 2009.

McDurmon, Joel, *Jesus Vs. Jerusalem*, (Powder Springs, GA., American Vision) 2012.

Meek, Charles S., *Christian Hope through Fulfilled Prophecy: An Exposition of Evangelical Preterism*, (Spicewood, Tx., Faith Facts Publishing) 2013.

185

Ogden, Arthur M., *Avenging the Apostles and Prophets*, (Pinson, Al., Ogden Publishing) 2006.

Preston, Don K., *Into All the World, Then Comes the End*, (Ardmore, Ok., JaDon Management Inc.) 1996.

The Last Days Identified, (Ardmore, Ok., JaDon Management Inc.) 2004

Blast From the Past: The Truth About Armageddon, (Ardmore, Ok., JaDon Management Inc.) 2005.

He Came As a Thief, (Ardmore, Ok., JaDon Management Inc.) 2008.

How Is This Possible?, (Ardmore, Ok., JaDon Management Inc.) 2009.

We Shall Meet Him in the Air, (Ardmore, Ok., JaDon Management Inc.) 2010.

Like Father, Like, On Clouds of Glory, (Ardmore, Ok., JaDon Management Inc.) 2010.

70 Weeks Are Determined for the Resurrection, (Ardmore, Ok., JaDon Management Inc.) 2010.

The End of Torah: At The Cross or AD 70?: A Debate On When the Law of Moses Passed, (Ardmore, Ok., JaDon Management Inc.) 2011.

Who Is This Babylon?, (Ardmore, Ok., JaDon Management Inc.) 2011.

Israel 1948: Countdown to Nowhere, (Ardmore, Ok., JaDon Management Inc.) 2011.

The Elements Shall Melt With Fervent Heat, (Ardmore, Ok., JaDon Management Inc.) 2012.

The End of the Law Torah to Telos Volume 1, (Ardmore, Ok., JaDon Management Inc.) 2012.

End Times Dilemma: Fulfilled or Future?: A Formal Debate Between a Full Preterist and a Dominionist, (Ardmore, Ok., JaDon Management Inc.) 2013.

AD 70: A Shadow of the "Real" End?, (Ardmore, Ok., JaDon Management Inc.) 2013.

The Hymenaean Heresy: Reverse the Charges!, (Ardmore, Ok., JaDon Management Inc.) 2014.

The Resurrection of the Dead: A Formal Debate – True Preterist – V-Postmillennialist, (Ardmore, Ok., JaDon Management Inc.) 2014.

Have Heaven and Earth Passed Away?: A Study of Matthew 5:17-18 and the Passing of the Law of Moses, (Ardmore, Ok., JaDon Management Inc.) 2015.

187

In Flaming Fire, (Ardmore, Ok., JaDon Management Inc.) 2015.

Elijah Has Come! A Solution to Romans 11:25-27: Torah To Telos: The Passing of the Law of Moses (Volume 3), (Ardmore, Ok., JaDon Management Inc.) 2016.

The Resurrection of Daniel 12: Future or Fulfilled?: Torah To Telos, The End of the Law of Moses (Volume 2), (Ardmore, Ok., JaDon Management Inc.) 2016.

Temple, Steve, *Who Was the Mother of Harlots?*, (Ardmore, Ok., JaDon Management Inc.) 2012.

Vincent, Joseph, *The Millennium, Past, Present Or Future?*, (Ardmore, Ok., JaDon Management Inc.) 2012.

CPSIA information can be obtained
at www.ICGtesting.com
Printed in the USA
LVOW13s2041221116
514101LV00021B/289/P